CERTAIN HOPE:

An Encouraging Word from Hebrews

Gary Holloway

HillCrest
PUBLISHING

Certain Hope

HillCrest
P U B L I S H I N G

1648 Campus Court
Abilene, TX 79601
www.hillcrestpublishing.com

Type Specifications: Headline set in Impact, 36 point, 80% width. Subhead set in Times Italics, 18 point. Body copy set in Times, 12 point. Endnotes set in Times, 10 point.

Printed in the United States of America

ISBN 0-89112-448-9

Library of Congress Card Number **98-89392**

1,2,3,4,5

To Tip Curd, Ralph Nance, and Hollis Todd:
the leaders of the Natchez Trace Church of Christ.

Contents

Dedication 3

Introduction 7

1 The Last Word 11
Many Voices 11
God Has Spoken 13
The Greatness of the Spokesman 14
The Last Word? 16

2 More Than an Angel 21
Contemporary vs. Biblical Angels 22
Greater Than Angels. 23
Don't Settle for Less 26
Pay Closer Attention 28

3 Brother 31
Brother Jesus 32
The Flesh-and-Blood Jesus 33
The Suffering Jesus 35
The Triumphant Jesus 38

4 Hard Hearts 41
Hard Hearts 41
Hardened by Sin 43
Heart Smart 45
Just Do It 48

5 Trying to Get Some Rest 51
Weary to the Bone 51
The Joy of Salvation 53
The Rest That Comes Through Work 55
How to Enter the Once-and-Future Rest 57
Hang in There, Rest is Coming 58

6 Help! 61
Help With Our Weaknesses 62
Help With Our Sins 65

Help With Obedience 66
Salvation Means Being Helped 68

7   To The Very End **71**
Will We Fall Away? 72
Better Things 75
Keep On To the End 78

8   Renegotiating the Contract **83**
The Old Deal 84
The New Deal 86
Don't Look Back 89

9   Once-For-All **93**
Christ's Sacrifice: Once for all 94
Death and Judgment: Once for all 97
Christ's Second Coming: Once for all 98
Life Between the Once-for-alls 99

10   Let Us... .... **103**
Let Us Draw Near to God 105
Let Us Hold Tight to Our Hope 107
Let Us Spur One Another On 109
Let Us Not Give Up Meeting Together 110
Receiving What God Has Promised 111

11   Family Portrait **113**
Our Family 113
Our Character 115
Our Endurance 118

12   A Consuming Fire **123**
The Fire That Punishes 124
The Fire that Disciplines 126
The Fire That Purifies 129
An Encouraging Word? 130

13   Last Words **133**
Love and Care for Others 133
Keep Marriage Holy 136
Trust God, Not Money 137
Remember Your Leaders 137
Trust Grace, Not Legalism 138
Offer the Sacrifices of Praise and Service 139
Rely on God 140

Introduction

Could you use a word of encouragement?

When my niece, Katie, was a baby and would begin to cry uncontrollably, her father, Rush, would burst out in song with the first words of a hymn, "Troublesome times are here..." I think he was on to something.

Sometimes we all need a word of encouragement. Troublesome times are here, and not just when the baby is crying. We face all kinds of trouble. There are ordinary troubles: nagging illnesses make us feel not quite ourselves; our jobs become boring and repetitive; we worry about our children; we don't feel appreciated.

Then there are real troubles, serious ones: the tumor is malignant; the company is downsizing and you lose your job; your single daughter is expecting; your parents have to move in with you; your faith is challenged and you begin to wonder if you've lost it altogether.

Then there are the troublesome times in which we live, times we cannot control. Like many of my generation who were raised in small towns and suburbs, I grew up in Mayberry, or rather, in Beaver Cleaver's neighborhood. I played outside with all the neighborhood kids and even went to their houses without my parents being alarmed. After all, everyone in our neighborhood was a Christian of some sort (well, except for the Jewish family around the corner and the one family down the street who didn't go to church anywhere). Even if they weren't devout Christians, they were good people, decent people. You could trust your kids would be O.K. at their houses.

Times have changed. We hear so much today about violence and abuse that we want to know a great deal about a family before we let our kids play with them. We don't let them play in the neighborhood after dark. We don't even walk in the neighborhood after dark. Our culture, our nation, seems to have changed for the worse, and no matter what politicians promise, they cannot deliver. Things don't get better.

How do we live as Christians in times like these? How do we live bold, confident lives in an age that is increasingly neutral or even hostile to Christian faith? How do we keep our faith and keep our children faithful in the face of the greed and violence of a culture rushing madly after pleasure?

What we need is a word of encouragement.

A Timely Word

This book provides that word—or rather, it points to a much older book that gives encouragement—the biblical book of Hebrews.

Hebrews is one of the neglected books of the New Testament. We neglect it, perhaps, because it speaks of things so foreign to our experience: sacrifices, high priests, tabernacles, and covenants. It tells stories of obscure characters like Melchizedek. We're not even sure what kind of biblical book this is. We place it with the epistles or letters, but it doesn't read like a letter. We don't even know who wrote it.

Why study such a strange book? Because we live in strange times—difficult times, troublesome times. We need strength. We want encouragement.

That's exactly what Hebrews supplies. Near the end of Hebrews, the author tells his readers, "I urge you, brothers, to bear with my word of encouragement, for I have written to you briefly" (13:22). The author of Hebrews writes to Christians who live in troublesome times. Their world, like ours, was increasingly hostile to

Christianity. They, too, feared for their children. They, too, faced sickness of body and soul.

Hebrews is written to encourage them—and us. All the things mentioned in Hebrews—angels, Moses, Melchizedek, priests, heroes, tabernacles, sacrifices, and covenants—are there to point us to the greatest encourager of all: Jesus Christ. No matter what we face individually or as the people of God, Christ has faced it before us. He is there as the pioneer of our faith, who blazes the trail for us. He is the champion who wins the victory for us. He is there, suffering with us in our hour of deepest despair. He is there, waiting for us to join him in glory.

No matter what we face, no matter what trouble comes, Jesus is always there for us. That is the message of Hebrews: a word of encouragement. Exactly what we need to hear.

1
The Last Word

In these last days he has spoken to us by his Son...
Hebrews 1:2

Not long after the demise of the Soviet Union, an elderly Russian woman came to America. One day she went for the first time to an American supermarket. Accustomed to long lines and food shortages, she entered the supermarket, saw fruits, vegetables, meats, and canned goods piled high on their shelves—and promptly fainted. She'd never seen so much food in one place. The choices were too much for her.

I've never fainted while grocery shopping, but I sometimes feel like this woman. There are always at least four kinds of oranges in our produce section along with some fruits and vegetables I've never seen before. The choices are staggering. I don't know what to pick.

The dizzying array of choices is also found outside of supermarkets. In the marketplace of ideas, we are faced with a bewildering array of choices—philosophies, values, and perspectives from a myriad of cultures. Which should we choose? What should we believe? To whom shall we listen?

Many Voices

We live in a pluralistic culture, a time when many voices clamor for our attention. Once I was returning from Europe on a flight to Houston. As we got off the plane and headed toward customs, I noticed a man in front of me with a rich, luxurious beard. He wore a turban. As we reached the signs that separated the passengers into "American Citizens" and "Foreign Nationals," the turbaned man went into the American citizens' line. A fellow in cowboy boots who was next to him said, "Hey, buddy, this line is for U.S. citizens." The man in the turban replied, "I am a U.S. citizen."

An embarrassing situation. Embarrassing, because we know that not all Americans look alike or think alike. We live in a country that is a melting-pot, a mosaic of cultures. Each culture brings its own insights and practices to enrich the fabric of American life.

If that is what is meant by pluralism, that various cultures in our country and our world each claim a particular viewpoint, then all should admit that pluralism is a true and fine thing.

However, pluralism has come to mean more than just difference and variety among peoples. It has come to mean there is no truth except what is true for me, and what is true for me might not be true for you. In this view, "truth" has no meaning except as shorthand for what an individual believes or what those in power say truth is.

Pluralism prizes tolerance above all virtues. But the tolerance it practices is not the love of neighbor that keeps one from persecuting those whose views are false. Instead pluralism claims to tolerate all beliefs, except those that actually claim to be true. To make a contemporary, "tolerant" person hopping mad, all you have to do is claim that a particular belief is true, no matter who believes it or disbelieves it.

This "tolerance" is illustrated by a television interview of Billy Graham conducted years ago by Johnny Carson. Carson praised Graham and his evangelistic work. He thought it was great, provided Graham "did not force his beliefs on me." The studio audience broke into loud applause at these words.

— only if [handwritten] *without arrogance and with love* [handwritten]

But if truth is truth, then we are not "forcing" it on people if we simply proclaim it as truth. And some truths call for a response, a change of life. It's that call to respond that many find offensive.

Here's the real question we face in all this talk of pluralism: is truth to be found in a plurality of voices or from one voice? Is "truth" merely our word for the way we feel at the moment? Is it to be found in the cacophony of voices that assault us each day? Or is there real truth, solid truth, from a completely reliable source outside ourselves?

God Has Spoken

Hebrews begins with the good news: there is real truth. God has not left us in the confusion of a myriad of voices, but he has spoken a clear word to us through his Son:

> In the past God spoke to our forefathers through the prophets at many times and in various ways, but in these last days, he has spoken to us by his Son....
>
> (Hebrews 1:1-2)

God never left his creation to find its way alone. From the beginning, even after humans sinned, he revealed himself to them through the prophets. The Old Testament tells stories of the many ways God spoke—burning bushes, smoke and lightning, dreams and visions, even still, small voices. God spoke clearly to his people, but not fully or finally. His final word comes through his Son. "The word became flesh and made his dwelling among us" (John 1:14).

Jesus is God in the flesh. When he speaks, we hear the voice of God. Here is truth. Here is certainty. We have confidence not in our ability to ferret truth from the competing voices around us, but in what Jesus says and who Jesus is.

The Greatness of the Spokesman

The writer of Hebrews highlights the importance of this sure word from God by focusing on the greatness of Jesus, God's Spokesman. In the words of what may have been an early Christian hymn, he describes the Son in seven ways.

1. The Son is heir of all things. We think of an heir as someone who will receive a legacy. In the Old Testament, the word is used a bit differently. It refers to one who takes permanent possession of what God has promised. Israel became the heir of the promised land when the land became theirs. In the same way, to say the Son is the heir of all things is to say that everything is permanently his. Jesus owns all of creation and if we remain faithful to him, we are heirs of the new creation (Romans 8:17).

2. Through the Son, God the Father created the universe. Not only do all things belong to Jesus, but he made all things in the beginning. The Son, God's last word to humanity, was also God's first Word, the Word that made the world. "Through him all things were made; without him nothing was made that has been made" (John 1:3; see also Colossians 1:15). Jesus speaks the truth about us and our world because he made the world in the beginning and all things are his.

3. The Son radiates God's glory. The glory of God refers both to his brightness and to his reputation. God is light and shines with a glory brighter than the sun. Jesus, the Son radiates (or reflects, as some translations say) that brightness and glory. God the Father deserves honor and glory as our Creator and Redeemer. The Son also deserves praise as Creator and Redeemer. Glory is a word that

describes the divine reality in the Bible. Jesus glows with that divine reality.

4. The Son is the exact representation of God's essence. The Son is the imprint (Greek, *charakter*) of God's very nature. The picture is of a metal stamp in hot wax. The stamp leaves an exact imprint in the wax. In the same way, the character of God is embedded in the person of Jesus. The Son is fully God as well as fully man.

5. The Son sustains all things by his powerful word. Not only did the Son make all things in the beginning, but he keeps the creation going. "In him all things hold together" (Colossians 1:17). The Son did not merely create the world and then leave it to run according to "the laws of nature." Instead, he is still intimately involved in his creation, working each moment to keep it together and support it.

6. The Son made purification for sins. "Purification" is a familiar word to readers of the Old Testament, where sins are purified through washing or through sacrifice. As we will see later in Hebrews, the Son is the ultimate sacrifice for our sins. This is the heart of the Christian message, the good news of Jesus Christ. God the Son himself, the one who made and sustains the universe, the one who radiates God's glory and bears the stamp of his nature, this great God became a man and died for our sins. Amazing!

7. The Son sat down at the right hand of God. Jesus the Son is vindicated by God at his resurrection. He appears to his disciples, then he ascends to be with the Father as he was before the beginning. More than that, he is given the place of honor at God's right hand because he has been obedient to the Father, obedient even to the cross. Jesus the Son now reigns with God eternally and the day is coming when every knee will bow to him:

> Therefore God also highly exalted him
> and gave him the name that is above every
> name,

so that at the name of Jesus every knee should
bend,
in heaven and on earth and under the earth,
and every tongue should confess
that Jesus Christ is Lord,
to the glory of God the Father.

(Philippians 2:10-11)

Thus the writer of Hebrews describes the Son: heir,
creator, sustainer, bearer of God's glory and nature,
sacrifice, omnipotent Lord. Why? Why does he tell us
these things we already know about Jesus the Son? What
difference does it make?

All the difference in the world. We are reminded
of the greatness of Jesus to assure us of the importance of
the message he brings. We are not left on our own without
a sure word from God. He has spoken! God has spoken
through his Son, who is God in the flesh. Jesus speaks
through his teachings. He speaks through the cross. He
speaks in the resurrection. He speaks from the right hand
of the Father. He speaks of love, forgiveness, mercy, and
new life. This great Son himself is the Word—the Word
of encouragement.

The Last Word?

Christians confess that Jesus is God's word to
humanity. What is scandalous in our society is that we
confess that he is God's last and final word. Many in our
time are willing to accept Jesus as a great moral teacher,
even as a prophet of God. They also believe Christianity
is one of the world's great religions. What offends them
is the suggestion that Christianity is the only true religion
or (to put it better) that salvation is to be found only in
Christ.

Yet that is what the Bible clearly says. Peter tells the Jewish leaders in Jerusalem, "Salvation is found in no one else, for there is no other name under heaven given to men by which we must be saved" (Acts 4:12). "No other name..." It sounds so exclusive, so intolerant.

But Jesus himself is as exclusive and intolerant. *but very forgiving*
Scripture records, "Jesus answered, 'I am the way and the truth and the life. No one comes to Father except through me'" (John 14:6). No one can come to the Father except through Jesus. He is not *a* way to God, he is *the* way: the only way, the only truth, and the only name that saves.

I don't have all the answers as to what that means. I'm not certain about those who have never heard the gospel. I am certain that the words of Jesus and Peter exclude an easy-going pluralism that accepts all statements and beliefs as equally true and equally false. There is truth. It is found in a person. His name is Jesus.

If we follow Jesus, that doesn't mean we have all the answers to life. It means he does. The great and ultimate truth is not found at the end of human investigation. It is a gift of God: the greatest gift of all.

The world we live in does not understand this. Perhaps there are some of us who are Christians and still do not understand. We might think truth is objective and impersonal. That may be true for some truth, but not for the greatest truth of all.

The tower that stands at the center of the University of Texas has these words inscribed on it: "You will know the truth and the truth will set you free." There is some irony in these words being at the center of a secular university. To most who pass by, the words imply that, given enough time, effort, and research, humans can find truth and set themselves free.

In their original context, those words have a quite different meaning. Jesus says them to those who would be his disciples:

To the Jews who had believed him, Jesus said, "If you hold to my teaching, you are really my disciples. Then you will know the truth and the truth will set you free."

(John 8:31-32)

We live in a confusing time. Many are lost in the fullest sense of the word: lost in a world with no signposts, no truth to guide them. The good news is this: there is a sure sign, a trustworthy guide, a certain truth. That truth is a person. He is the Word. He is the Way.

And yet this is not good news to everyone. Not all will accept this truth. Not all will hear the Word. Even those of us who wish to hear cannot come to this truth on our own terms. The voices of our age are at times so persuasive, so interesting, and so novel that we must work hard to hear the voice of Jesus. We need disciplined ears and disciplined lives. We must become his disciples, hold to his teaching, and cling to him in a world of confusing and conflicting voices.

As we saw above, the great description of the Son given in Hebrews may have been from an early Christian hymn. This gives us insight into how we should hear God's last word to us. Jesus the Word is not to be grasped just by the mind. He is heard by heart, soul, and body: by all that we are. When we truly hear him, we break out in songs of praise for who he is: God's last and best word to his troubled world; God's loving word to us; truth made flesh; the living Word.

In the words of an ancient hymn:

Jesus, thou joy of loving hearts,
Thou fount of life, Thou light of men,
From all the bliss that earth imparts
We turn unfilled to Thee again.

Thy truth unchanged hath ever stood;
Thou savest those that on Thee call;
To them that seek Thee Thou art good;
To them that find Thee, all in all.

We can praise Jesus with old words or new. The point is that he becomes our all in all, God's last, best, and final word.

Can you hear him?

Questions for Discussion

1. What do you understand the term "pluralism" to mean? Is pluralism in this sense a biblical concept or not?

2. Is there "real truth" for everyone or is there only what is true for me and what is true for you?

3. Are Christians arrogant when they claim salvation is only in Jesus?

4. What about those who sincerely follow other world religions such as Islam, Hinduism and Buddhism? Can't God save them without Christ?

5. What statements about the greatness of Jesus would you add to the seven in Hebrews 1?

2
More Than an Angel

Let all God's angels worship him.

Hebrews 1:6

Americans have gone angel crazy.

There are movies about angels, television shows built around angels, and over three hundred books in print about angels. Angels show up on greeting cards and stationary. Portraits of angels hang on the walls of posh businesses and fashionable homes. There are even dozens of web-sites about angels.

outdated

Why the explosion of interest in angels? Is this a sign of a spiritual renewal in America? Or is it a sign of spiritual deception? Perhaps a bit of both.

On the one hand, the current popularity of angels shows that Americans are not as secular as we once thought. Most of the current stories about angels revolve around their roles as protectors. A car skids completely out of control, careening from side to side across the expressway, yet the driver and her three small children escape unharmed. Why? "I felt a presence with me," the driver says. A guardian angel? Others tell similar stories of strangers coming to their aid and then disappearing. Of lights leading them through the woods when they were lost. Of money coming in unmarked envelopes in the mail when they were down to their last dime.

Angels?

Perhaps. One thing these stories show for sure is that contemporary people no longer trust that science or the government or American ingenuity will solve all their problems. We need a higher power.

That recognition is certainly a step in the right direction for our society. However, the danger is that we will settle for a higher power, not the Highest Power. We might even settle for less than biblical angels.

Contemporary vs. Biblical Angels

Contemporary angels in television and movies are almost always portrayed by extremely attractive actors. They are always gentle, smiling, and upbeat. The most popular artistic portraits of angels are of cherubs, described by some as "baby angels." These angels have all the innocence and beauty of infants, along with supernatural power. When one sees portraits of these angels, one wants to say, "How sweet."

However, when people in the Bible see angels, they don't say, "How sweet." Instead, they fall on the ground with fear and trembling. Zechariah sees the angel Gabriel and is terrified and overwhelmed with fear (Luke 1:12). Tough Roman soldiers guarding the tomb of Jesus see an angel and are so afraid of him they faint dead away (Matthew 28:4). Cherubs in scripture are not baby angels, but terrifying creatures who guard the very throne of God (see Ezekiel 10; Isaiah 37:16).

Angels in the Bible are powerful and scary. After all, they come from the presence of the Almighty God. By contrast, in the contemporary mind, angels are warm and fuzzy. Why the difference? People are comfortable with the thought of angels who are never demanding but always there to help us whenever we are in need. They are much less interested in angels that come from the throne of an all-powerful, demanding Lord of the Universe.

The current interest in angels has a downside. While Christians welcome the interest in the supernatural, we also realize that an obsession with angels can blind one to the Lord of the angels. Our society's preoccupation with angelic messengers may be a way of avoiding the message, a message from the one who is greater than angels: greater, more frightening, more demanding—and more giving.

Greater Than Angels

We are not the first generation to pay too much attention to angels. Or rather, to pay too little attention to the one greater than angels. The readers of Hebrews were also tempted to forget the one who is more than an angel: the only Son of God.

Having praised the Son as creator, sustainer, and redeemer, the writer of Hebrews lists three reasons why Jesus is superior to angels.   *See Heb 2:7, 9*

1. He has a superior name. Names imply little in our culture. Many of us don't even know what our names mean. Names are just labels for people. We don't think of their significance. Indeed, most of us would agree with Shakespeare, "What's in a name? That which we call a rose / by any other name would smell as sweet."

In some cultures, names are indicative of a person's character. The name is the essence of the self. Native Americans were given names like Running Buffalo, Wise Elk, or Sitting Bull, not because the names were quaint, but because they captured the personality of the individual.

It's the same in the Bible. Names mean something. When they said "Abraham," they thought, "Father of a Multitude." Isaac was "Laughter." Jacob was "Heel-Grabber" (Genesis 25:26). A name was more than a label to them; it was a badge of character that was to be worn with pride.

The greatest name of all was the Name of the Lord. In Hebrew, this name was probably pronounced as "Yahweh." We're not sure of the pronunciation because the Jews eventually thought the name was so holy that they would not pronounce it. Instead, they used the word "Lord" or even simply said, "Name." "Blessed be the Name" meant "Praise be to God." The Name was as holy and was to be as respected as God himself.

So it is significant that Jesus is given a name that is superior to the angels. What is that name? The name is Son.

> For to which of the angels did God ever say,
> "You are my Son;
> today I have become your Father?"
> Or again,
> "I will be his Father,
> and he will be my Son?"
>
> (Hebrews 1:5)

These two rhetorical questions are quotations from Psalm 2:7 and 2 Samuel 7:14. The obvious answer to the questions is, "God never called the angels 'sons.'" However, there are several Old Testament passages that do call the angels "sons of God" (Job 1:6; 2:1; 38:7; Psalms 29:1; 89:6). Is this a contradiction? No. Angels are called sons of God, and Christians are also called children of God. But neither we nor angels are sons in the same way that Jesus is Son. Jesus is uniquely the "one and only Son" (John 3:16). As the writer of Hebrews has already said, Jesus the Son is the exact representation of God's being. He is God himself.

This makes the Son infinitely superior to the angels. He is God; they are not. He is Creator; they are

2 PET 2:10 celestial beings, vs. angels
2 PET 2:14 angels sinned?

creations. Angels are glorious super-human beings, but they don't hold a candle to the glory of the Son. His name is obviously superior.

2. The angels worship the Son. The second indicator that Jesus is superior to angels is that they worship him.

> And again, when God brings his firstborn into
> the world, he says,
> "Let all God's angels worship him."

> (Hebrews 1:6)

When Jesus is born, the heavenly host of angels rejoice and praise God (Luke 2:13-14). This may be the worship the writer of Hebrews has in mind. However, it is more likely that the phrase "when God brings his firstborn into the world" refers not to the birth of the incarnate Son but to the Son's entry into "the world to come" (Hebrews 2:5). The Son has entered the world of glory. Now seated on the right hand of the Father, he receives glory and honor from the angels in heaven.

Either on earth or in heaven, the point remains the same: the angels worship Jesus. Lower beings always worship higher ones. Thus, Jesus the Son is superior to the angels. They themselves recognize his superiority by bowing before him in worship.

3. The Son reigns, but angels serve. Two verses speak of the role of angels as servants:

> In speaking of the angels he says,
> "He makes his angels winds,
> his servants flames of fire."

> (Hebrews 1:7)

> Are not all angels ministering spirits sent to serve
> those who will inherit salvation?

> (Hebrews 1:14)

Angels are servants by nature. They were created by God to serve him. What's more, angels even serve human beings, "those who will inherit salvation." It makes no sense to give too much glory to angels, because they are sent by God to serve us.

It also makes no sense to glorify them more than or as much as we glorify the Son. While they were created to serve, the Son is himself the Creator (Hebrews 1:10-12). They serve but he reigns eternally (Hebrews 1:8). As the servant is not above his master (Matthew 10:24), so angels cannot be superior to Jesus the Son.

[handwritten: ✗ Christ served as well, Service was central to His ministry (Mark 10:45)]

Don't Settle for Less

Why does the writer of Hebrews go to so much trouble to belabor the obvious? Surely his readers know as well as we do that Jesus is greater than the angels. Why *[handwritten: Heb 2:7,9]* go to such elaborate lengths to prove Jesus is superior?

Because his readers were tempted to settle for angels and neglect the Son of God. Are we any better? Isn't part of the angel craze in our time a way to say "Yes" to the supernatural but "No, thanks" to Christianity? Are we not tempted to settle for angelic help whenever we need it instead of thirsting for a relationship with the Lord of the angels?

I am reminded of the story of Jacob and Esau in the Old Testament. Esau had been out hunting, unsuccessfully it appears, and he returns home famished. He can smell the savory stew his brother Jacob has on the fire. "Give me some stew, I'm starving," he tells his brother Jacob. But Jacob demands a price. He wants the lion's share of the inheritance, Esau's birthright. Esau is so hungry he sells his birthright for a pot of stew. "So Esau despised his birthright," (Genesis 25:34).

[handwritten: Gen 25 v.32. Perhaps this with Esau means that he will die first (prior to Jacob), so what is the value of a birthright?]

How stupid to sell one's future prosperity for a pot of thin stew. But are we any better? Have we not been driven by immediate desires? Have we not satisfied our present hungers by ignoring what is best for us long term? Do we not at times settle for less? Esau's attitude was, "Just help me now and let the future take care of itself." Sound familiar?

Isn't that partly what is behind the current angel craze? We want supernatural help; we want angels to protect us in traffic; we want them to keep us safe from crime; we want them to find us when we are lost. We want them at our beck and call. What we may not want is a relationship that demands something—everything— from us. Like Esau, we may be settling for less.

How is this settling for less? Because we are failing to see that there is one greater than angels. He does more than protect us in traffic; he protects us from the evil one. He not only keeps us safe from crime; he turns the sinner from doing wrong. He found us when we were lost. He saves by his own blood.

We dare not miss him by settling for angels. We leave after the overture, and think we've heard the concert. We hear the National Anthem and think we've seen the ball game. We see a clown and think we've experienced the whole circus.

We want angels to help us. "What's wrong with that?" you ask. Nothing. They are "sent to serve for the sake of those who are to inherit salvation" (Hebrews 1:14). That's amazing—that angels serve us. What's more amazing, even unbelievable, is that the Almighty Creator, the Sustainer of the Universe, the Son of God himself "did not come to be served, but to serve, and to give his life a ransom for many" (Mark 10:45).

The Son of God wants to help you. Don't settle for less.

Pay Closer Attention

With the amazing news that the Son himself serves us comes a corresponding warning: do not neglect his service. If angels claim our attention in movies, books, and television, how much more should we hear the voice of Jesus?

We must pay more careful attention, therefore, to what we have heard, so that we do not drift away. For if the message spoken by angels was binding, and every violation and disobedience received its just punishment, how shall we escape if we ignore such a great salvation?

(Hebrews 2:1-3)

"How shall we escape...?" The words seem harsh, even ominous. Is this good news, a word of encouragement? Yes, for it reminds us of what is at stake: our salvation, our eternal happiness, our relationship with God, our very selves.

The contrast here is with the Old Testament, the message spoken by angels (Deuteronomy 33:2; Acts 7:38, 53; Galatians 3:19), and the new covenant brought by Christ. Under the Old Testament, one had to take God's message seriously. If one did not, there were consequences to pay. One could be fined, beaten, and even stoned to death for not keeping the Law.

We see such an arrangement as harsh and demanding. The writer of Hebrews reminds us that our message of salvation is greater than the Old Testament message. Our word from God is the Word of God—the Son of God. Should we not take his message more seriously, not because we fear punishment, but because we love the Messenger who gave his life for us? He is God's final Word to us. If we don't pay attention to that Word, if we ignore it, there is no where else to turn. If we neglect Jesus, punishment is the only alternative.

Encouragement

What is it that threatens our faith? Persecution? Not likely. Unbelievers? I doubt an atheist will talk us out of our belief. Hard times? Perhaps, but we know they can also strengthen us.

Prosperity may be our greatest threat. Our faith grows weak when things go well. Day follows day, week follows week, and nothing seems to change. "Things are great," we say. And so they are. Yet the day-to-day path of obedience is unexciting; it's boring, long, and hard.

We are not tempted to give up our faith in some dramatic flourish. We do not curse God. We don't stop coming to church. But we begin to do what Hebrews warns us about: we pay less attention to our salvation. We drift, neglect, and ignore.

If we drift and ignore we will not escape our just punishment. This warning is ominous and scary. When angels appear, they frighten those who see them. When Jesus appears, it is even more frightening. Yet the angels have a word of encouragement. Whenever they appear, they say, "Do not be afraid!" How much more does the frightening Jesus say, "Don't be afraid!" He came to save and serve, not to frighten. We should fear only if we neglect his salvation.

So what do we do about his great salvation? Listen up! Pay attention! Give some effort! This is the encouraging word of Hebrews. The one we serve is greater than angels. He deserves our attention, our focus, our effort. He deserves all we are and all we have. He deserves it because of who he is, the eternal Son of God. He deserves it because of what he has done.

He served us first, providing a great salvation—the greatest ever. Don't settle for angels. Don't settle for less.

Questions for Discussion

1. How do you explain the recent explosion of interest in angels?

2. In what ways are the contemporary views of angels different from biblical descriptions of them?

3. Are names significant in our culture? How about titles? What are some important names and titles for angels? For Jesus?

4. What does it mean to say, "Settling for angels is settling for less?"

5. What are some signs that we might be drifting away from or neglecting our salvation?

3
Brother

So Jesus is not ashamed to call them brothers.
Hebrews 2:11

My brothers and I have nothing in common. They drive big trucks and like going to tractor pulls. I prefer a compact car and going to the movies. They work with their hands and can fix anything around the house. I can screw in a light bulb, given enough time and instructions. They work in factories and out-of-doors. I sit in an office and grade papers. They like to fish and hunt. I read books. We have nothing in common.

And yet, of course, we do. We have a collection of shared experiences. When we get together we share stories of times in the past: memories, family vacations, favorite Christmas gifts. We reminisce about Grandpa Holloway dancing at the family reunion, about the time the bird flew into my plate of food on a camping trip, about the stories Papa Perkins told. We have those memories in common.

In some ways, I'm not very close to my brothers. We have little in common. We don't get to spend much time with each other. In another way, we are as close as we can be. After all, we are brothers. We share a common father. It is our love for him and for Mom that binds us together. We share the same flesh and blood.

Brother Jesus

Jesus is more than an angel. He is Lord, Savior, God himself in the flesh. We are comfortable with these images of Jesus. They show up in our conversations, in our hymns, and in our prayers. We fall before Jesus as our Creator, our King, and our Redeemer. But he is more than that; he calls himself our brother.

"Brother Jesus." It sounds somewhat strange. There are few hymns that call him "brother." I rarely hear Christians call Jesus "brother." Why? Why are we more comfortable describing him as "Lord" than as "brother?"

Maybe it's because we know who we are. We know ourselves, in our worst moments, as sinful, cruel, and selfish. "My brother, Jesus" sounds too familiar. It drags Jesus down to our level. It makes him one of us. We are embarrassed to use such language. But Jesus is not embarrassed!

> Both the one who makes men holy and those who are made holy are of the same family. So Jesus is not ashamed to call them brothers. He says, "I will declare your name to my brothers; in the presence of the congregation I will sing your praises."

> (Hebrews 2:11-12)

Jesus is our brother. We are part of the same family. But how can this be when he is the holy Son of God and we are sinful, fallen people? It seems clear at first that we have little in common with our brother Jesus. He is sinless. We are not.

Yet it is the same with Jesus as with our earthly brothers. What makes us brothers is not that we act or think or do things alike. What makes us brothers is a common Father. With God as our Father, Jesus is our brother. We share the same family experiences and memories as the Son of God. So, we too are sons and daughters of God, no matter how little we think we have in common with him. And the truth is he has a great deal in common with us. We even share the same flesh and blood.

The Flesh-and-Blood Jesus

When doctors need an organ for transplant, where do they first turn? To the patient's brothers and sisters. Why? Because we're more likely to donate a kidney to our brother or sister than to a complete stranger? Perhaps. But the main reason is that an organ from a brother or sister is more likely to be a match in tissue. The transplant will "take" and there will be less chance of rejection.

It's the same way with Jesus. To help us he had to match us. He had to be our brother. He had to share our flesh and blood.

A few years ago, pop singer Joan Osborne upset some religious folks by singing "One of Us" by songwriter Eric Bazilian. The song asks:

What if God were one of us?
Just a slob like one of us?
Just a stranger on a bus, trying to make his way home...

Some saw the song as blasphemous, lowering God to the level of the worst of humanity: "...just a slob like one of us."

But isn't that the heart of the Gospel? Isn't that the amazing, shocking message we proclaim? "The Word became flesh..." (John 1:14). The Son of God, God's last word to humanity, became one of us.

Or did he? Was he really like us? Completely human? In the early church there were some Christians who just could not bring themselves to believe that Jesus was really one of us. They could believe Jesus looked like a human being, but refused to accept that he could actually be hungry and thirsty, that he could be tempted to sin, or that he could suffer pain and despair. These Christians were called "docetists" (from the Greek *dokeo*, to seem) because they said Jesus only seemed to have a body.

Such thoughts are strange to us. I don't know any Christians today who would deny Jesus had a real body. Such an idea seems laughable. Yet, many Christians I have known find it difficult, even impossible, to think Jesus was completely human as we are. If he was, then he woke up some mornings and didn't want to get out of bed. He got cranky when he was hungry. He had his bad days. At times, if just for a moment, he thought about disobeying God. Isn't that what temptation means?

He was a slob like one of us. Such ideas seem shocking. Yet they are the heart of the word of encouragement from the writer of Hebrews:

> Since the children have flesh and blood, he too shared in their humanity so that by his death he might destroy him who has the power of death—that is, the devil—and free those who all their lives were held in slavery by their fear of death.

(Hebrews 2:14-15)

God sent his Son to die for our sins. That is the heart of the gospel. But he sent him as one who was fully human, flesh and blood, one of us. Why? Because only one who fully experienced death could free us from death. Only one who truly suffered could end our suffering. Only one who was really tempted could help us in temptation. "Because he himself suffered when he was tempted, he is able to help those who are being tempted" (Hebrews 2:18). Only a powerful God could save us; only a sympathetic man could save us. Jesus the complete Savior, is both.

The Suffering Jesus

We know Jesus came to suffer for our sins. Many of us have heard that all our lives. In fact, we've heard it so often that it no longer astounds us. We rightly associate that suffering with the cross. "God demonstrates his love for us in this: While we were still sinners, Christ died for us" (Romans 5:8).

But the cross wasn't the first time Jesus suffered. The writer of Hebrews reminds us that Jesus suffered temptation before he suffered death:

> In bringing many sons to glory, it was fitting that God, for whom and through whom everything exists, should make the author of their salvation perfect through suffering.
>
> For this reason he has to be made like his brothers in every way, in order that he might become a merciful and faithful high priest in service to God, and that he might make atonement for the sins of the people. Because he suffered when he was tempted, he is better able to help those who are being tempted.
>
> (Hebrews 2:10, 17-18)

Jesus went to the cross. There, we have no trouble believing he is flesh and blood. He suffered as any human would. Nails pierced flesh, blood flowed, the shock of pain followed. Jesus cried out in agony and despair. The Son of God is one of us, and he endured all this for us. He is the high priest who offered himself.

We have no trouble accepting a Jesus who suffers for us, but what about a Jesus who was tempted for us? We all know by experience what it means to be tempted. You are married, but your husband does not appreciate you or understand you. Another man is warmer, kinder, and more attentive. He thinks you hung the moon. As a Christian, you know you should keep your marriage vows, but an inner voice says, "Leave that loser of a husband. Go with the man who loves you and will make you happy." At least part of you wants to hear that voice. That's temptation.

Or you're a single guy who's been dating a girl for quite some time. Your sexual desire is strong. You think about her all the time. You know you should save sex for marriage, but you think, "What's the harm? God wouldn't give me such strong desires and then expect me to deny them. It's just not natural." That's temptation.

Or you sit at a desk performing one of the most hateful tasks of life: filling out the income tax form. When you get to the bottom line, you can't believe how much you owe in addition to how much you've had deducted from your paychecks. "It's not fair," you say. All you have to do is inflate a few deductions. Chances are you won't get caught. The government takes too much of our money anyway. That's temptation.

We could multiply the examples indefinitely. We know what temptation is. We know our own inner cravings, our hidden thoughts, our selfish desires. We know what we are when the masks of respectability and religion are stripped away. There's a darkness in the depths of our hearts. No matter how much we fight that darkness, no matter how many times we pledge to be better, temptation comes. And we give in. It's only human.

Jesus was human. He was tempted, like us. Can we really accept that?

Can you believe that Jesus, the Son of God, had the same enticing thoughts we have? That he struggled, as we do, to fight the darkness that threatens to rule? Did Jesus hear the voices we hear? "Go on," the voices say. "What's the harm? No one will know..." Did part of him want to follow those voices?

If we believe the Bible, we have to answer, "Yes." Jesus was really tempted. He suffered on the cross, but first he suffered as he struggled with right and wrong.

Isn't temptation always a form of suffering? Sometimes it actually hurts as we fight the evil inclinations of our heart. Jesus is flesh and blood. His flesh is torn by the nails of the cross, but before that his spirit is torn by temptation of the devil.

Jesus was tempted. He is human. It's not wrong to be tempted, but it is wrong to give in to temptation. At every fork in the road, no matter how painful the decision might be, Jesus made the right choice.

We, however, don't always make the right choice. We give in to temptation—we sin. The good news is that Jesus died to atone for our sins. More good news is that he is there to help us when we are tempted. He knows the power of temptation. He heard the voices that said, "Go ahead and do it." He felt the compulsion to turn away from God. He fought the compulsion, talked back to the voices, and triumphed over their power. He is there to do the same in us. Because he suffered temptation, he stands with us when we are tempted. He fights for us.

Hebrews says that makes Jesus the "author of salvation" (2:10). The word translated "author" means one who is a leader and who begins something. Some translations use "pioneer." Jesus blazed the trail of our salvation, cutting through the tangled underbrush of temptation so our way would be clear. He suffered so we might not. Perhaps the word "champion" best describes what Hebrews means. Jesus is our champion. He fought in our place and beat temptation. By beating it, he weakened its power over us.

Maybe you remember being bullied by older kids. They knocked you down, bloodied your nose, and took your lunch money. No matter how hard you tried, you couldn't out run them or out fight them.

But your big brother could. He heard what was happening and one day he caught those bullies after school. This time they went away with bloody noses and a warning from your brother, "Leave my little brother alone or you'll be sorry!"

Jesus is our brother. He's not ashamed to call us his brothers and sisters. He's even proud to do so. He is our big brother who fought Satan and won. He got the devil off our backs, and stands there beside us to defend us whenever Satan shows his ugly face again. Still, at times we try to fight Satan on our own, without Jesus' help. We always fail. But our big brother Jesus is always there to bind our wounds and forgive. He fights for us; he suffers with us; he suffers for us.

The Triumphant Jesus

Jesus knows what it's like to fight Satan. He had his own nose bloodied by temptation. He had his body broken on a tree, but he won the battle. Because he won, God has crowned him victor.

> But we see Jesus, who was made a little lower than the angels, now crowned with glory and honor because he suffered death, so that by the grace of God he might taste death for everyone.

> (Hebrews 2:9)

What problems do you face? Are you suffering in pain? Brother Jesus suffered too. Do you struggle with temptation? So did brother Jesus, and he overcame it. Are you at the end of your rope, unable to face one more day, yet afraid to die? Brother Jesus is there to help. He even triumphed over death.

And we share in his victory. Brother Jesus won a hard-fought battle, a flesh-and-blood struggle. Because he won, God crowned him victor and gave him glory and honor. If we keep up the fight, if we continue to struggle, if we cry out for our older brother to defend us, then he always hears, always defends, always wins.

The apostle Paul knew what it was like to fight battles. He fought against the power of temptation, the pain of persecution, and the anxiety of ministry. At the end of his life he could say, "I have fought the good fight" (2 Timothy 4:7). But he knew he did not fight it alone. "I have been crucified with Christ and I no longer live, but Christ lives in me" (Galatians 2:20). "I can do everything through him who gives me strength" (Philippians 4:13). "The Lord will rescue me from every evil attack and will bring me safely to his heavenly kingdom" (2 Timothy 4:18). Paul knew his brother Jesus had fought for him. Would fight for him. He trusted Jesus would bring the crown of victory (2 Timothy 4:8).

The readers of Hebrews knew what it was like to be bullied by Satan. That fight only promised to get worse. "In your struggle against sin, you have not yet resisted to the point of shedding your blood" (Hebrews 12:4). Not yet, but that day was coming soon. Where do we focus when we struggle with sin? What do we see? Pain? Suffering? Overwhelming odds? Certain defeat?

"But we see Jesus," Hebrews says.

Do you see him? Can you see him as your flesh-and-blood brother? Do you trust him to fight the bullies in your life? Can you see him as one of us? Can you see him exalted in glory?

If so, the encouraging word is this: through him God will bring many children to glory (Hebrews 2:10). Just as he became one of us, so someday we will be like our brother Jesus. He is the champion who brings us to victory.

Questions for Discussion

1. Why is it we don't often call Jesus "brother"?

2. In what ways was Jesus like us? Was he ever cranky, irritable and in a bad mood?

3. Was Jesus really tempted as we are? Could he have sinned? Did part of him want to do wrong?

4. Was Jesus in any way different from us as humans?

5. What does it mean to call Jesus our champion? How does he fight for us?

4
Hard Hearts

See to it, brothers, that none of you has a sinful, unbelieving heart that turns away from the living God.

Hebrews 3:12

You've seen the ads on TV and read the magazine articles: heart disease is the number one killer of Americans. We hear constant reminders today to be "heart-smart." Many products promise to help us in that quest. There are low-fat—or even fat-free—ice cream, cookies, cakes, and pies. For breakfast you can eat low-fat bacon, eggs with no cholesterol, and waffles with reduced-calorie syrup. With the explosion of heart-healthy foods comes an equal increase in the popularity of exercise machines. These promise to tone your body, lower your risk of a heart attack, and help you lose weight, all with minimal effort. Just a few minutes each day.

We know what we should do to be heart-smart: eat less and exercise more. But many of us live dangerously by eating anything we want, exercising only when we feel like it, and not worrying about the consequences. We have always been healthy, so we take our health for granted. Someday, it'll catch up to us.

Hard Hearts

It's dangerous and foolish to neglect the health of our physical hearts. It is even more so to neglect our spiritual hearts. Yet many of God's people have done just that. To encourage his Christian readers to pay attention to their spiritual hearts, the writer of Hebrews quotes Psalm 95. The Psalmist urges his generation not to be like their hard-hearted ancestors who perished in the wilderness, recalling the story of the spies in Numbers 13-14. Thus we are encouraged by reading one biblical book (Hebrews) that quotes another (Psalms) that is based on still a third (Numbers):

> So, as the Holy Spirit says:
>
> Today, if you hear his voice, do not harden your hearts as you did in the rebellion,during the time of testing in the desert, where your fathers tested and tried me and for forty years saw what I did. That is why I was angry with that generation, and I said, 'Their hearts are always going astray, and they have not known my ways.' So I declared on oath in my anger, 'They shall never enter my rest.'
>
> (Hebrews 3:7-11)

Perhaps you remember the biblical story. God sent ten plagues on the Egyptians to convince them to let his people go. Through Moses, God had delivered the children of Israel out of slavery and led them to the border of Canaan, the promised land. "Promised land" was no mere cliché, but literal truth. The Israelites conquest of the land was as sure as the promises of God.

Before they entered the promised land, the Lord told Moses to send twelve men "to spy out the land of Canaan" (Numbers 13:2). They were to report on the number of the inhabitants, the fortifications of their cities, and the richness of their soil.

They were in full agreement on what they saw: Canaan was a rich land, "flowing with milk and honey."

But the inhabitants of the land were strong and their cities were well fortified. Where the spies disagreed was in their interpretation of these facts. The vast majority of them, ten of twelve, were frightened by what they saw. Convinced they could not conquer the land, they called the Israelites to return to Egypt—back to slavery!

But two of the spies, Caleb and Joshua, believed God was stronger than the largest Canaanite and he could conquer the most heavily fortified city. "Let's go up at once and occupy it," they said. "If the Lord is pleased with us, he will lead us into that land, a land flowing with milk and honey, and will give it to us" (Numbers 14:8).

The people followed the majority. They refused to trust God to give them the land. Their hearts were hard. As a result, God decided to start over with the next generation. He made the Israelites wander in the wilderness for forty years. No one of that generation except Caleb, Joshua, and their families entered the promised land.

Hardened by Sin

Why does the writer of Hebrews tell such an old story? He's writing to Christians long after the time of Moses. How can we relate to such an old story? We don't plan to enter the promised land.

Or do we? Isn't there another, better promised land for God's people? Doesn't he promise that we will see him face-to-face and live with him forever? Don't we face the same decision the ancient Israelites faced? Will we look at the obstacles of life or at the promises of God? Do we believe him or are our hearts hard? Hebrews warns:

> See to it, brothers, that none of you has a sinful, unbelieving heart that turns away from the living God. But encourage one another daily, as long as

it is called Today, so that none of you may be
hardened by sin's deceitfulness.

(Hebrews 3:12-13)

Sin fools us. It deceives. How? In the same way it
deceived the Israelites long ago. God had led them out of
Egypt, delivering them from enemies much stronger than
the Canaanites. He'd cared for them through the
wilderness. He had led them to the promised land. But at
the border of the promised land, at the very edge of
enjoying the greatest blessing from God, the Israelites lose
faith. Sin deceives them, convincing them that God could
not or would not give them the victory.

Are we not exactly in the same spot? One of my
favorite hymns, by Thomas Grinfield, says:

O how kindly hast Thou led me,
Heavenly Father, day by day;
Found my dwelling, clothed and fed me,
Furnished friends to cheer my way.

God has led us kindly in the past. He's blessed us
above what we can imagine. He's brought us safely out
of terrible situations. He's given us food, warm houses,
clothes, friends, and family.

In return, we say to God, "What have you done
for me, lately?" Oh, we wouldn't say it out loud. We're
much too pious for that. We wouldn't even think it, at
least not in those terms. But by our actions, we question
God's care for us. We "test and try" him as Israel did
(Hebrews 3:9). At the root of such unbelief is ingratitude.
We take his blessings so much for granted that we come
to think we have earned them ourselves. We trust ourselves
for the easy things in life, but fail to trust God when things
get difficult.

Testing God in this way puts him in a no-win
situation. Our daughter gets cancer, so we blame God.
After all, the innocent are not supposed to suffer. Then,

our daughter gets better, so we thank the doctors and the modern medicine that makes her well. We blame God for evil but do not give him credit for good. No matter what he does, God can't win. Our hearts are hard.

A hard heart is not a physical problem; it is a spiritual one. In Scripture, the heart is the seat of the emotions, the reservoir of thought, and the site of the will. The heart is the center of our being, what we are deep down inside. It's what gives us character and makes us unique.

Sin is heart trouble of the worst kind. Sin deceives us into thinking that God will not continue to bless. It hardens our heart to the constant goodness of God. It makes us doubt the tender mercy of the living God and turns us from him. There's no more serious threat than this kind of heart disease.

It was the sin of Israel in the wilderness. Hundreds of years later, it was the disease the Psalmist warned against. Over a thousand years after that, the writer of Hebrews was still sounding the warning. Two thousand years later, we must hear it, too. One thing never changes about human nature: we live in constant danger of developing hard hearts.

Heart Smart

What can we do to keep from being hard-hearted? Is there a prevention plan? The encouraging word from Hebrews is, "Yes, there is."

Step one is to encourage one another.

> But encourage one another daily, as long as it is called today....

> (Hebrews 3:13)

Many of us avoid physical exercise, even though it's good for our hearts. We avoid it because it's painful, repetitive, and boring. But exercise becomes much easier when done with someone else. We play racquetball, go to aerobics class, or pump iron at the health club, and time flies because others work out with us.

Spiritual exercise is the same. We need encouragement from others to keep our hearts from hardening. Worship should be focused on the living God, but we come together to worship. Bible study takes on a new dimension in small groups. Things happen when Christians pray together. In all these activities and more, we are encouraging one another spiritually.

And that encouragement should happen daily. How often have you begun an exercise program and then stopped? Why? Isn't it because you got busy and skipped a day? Then the next day you didn't exercise because you really didn't feel like it. The third day, none of your friends called to invite you to work out with them. Before you knew it, weeks had passed since you'd exercised. It's the same with spiritual exercise. We need it daily. We need others to encourage us daily. Have you been encouraged by someone lately? Have you encouraged someone today?

Step two in our spiritual fitness program is to build our stamina.

> We have come to share in Christ if we hold firmly till the end the confidence we had at first.

> (Hebrews 3:14)

In sporting terms, it's not how you start, it's how you finish. The Christian race is not a sprint, but a marathon. Do you remember the day you made the commitment to follow Christ? Do you remember the joy? The feeling of forgiveness? The confidence you had that you were right with God? Then hold on to that confidence. That's good advice to any distance runner: "Hold on." No matter what terrors we face, they should not shake the confidence we have in Christ. That confidence, that faith, must be exercised each day if we are to keep our hearts right before God.

Step three in our spiritual "heart-smart" program is to listen to the Great Physician.

> Today if you hear his voice, do not harden your hearts as you did in the rebellion.

> (Hebrews 3:15)

All exercise programs have fine print that says, "Consult your physician before beginning this program." Spiritual exercise is conducted under the care of the Great Physician, Jesus. Indeed, listening to his advice, hearing his voice, is in itself the whole of spiritual exercise. We hear Jesus as we pray and meditate on his word. To hear Jesus is to follow him, to obey, to trust. It is the antidote to the spiritual blindness and unbelief that the writer of Hebrews calls "hardness of heart."

Thus to keep our hearts healthy before God, we encourage one another and we build the stamina of our faith. We keep at our spiritual exercises even when they seem boring and painful. No pain, no gain. Yet this process is not completely in our own hands. We cannot make ourselves spiritually healthy by our power alone. Faith comes at the end of struggle and strife. It also comes as the free gift of God.

God has a magic pill for our spiritual hearts. It opens the arteries of faith that have been clogged by fears and doubts. It keeps our hearts strong and warm. That magic dose is the voice of God himself—the Word of God. His name is Jesus. If we listen to him, we will hear that marvelous message of grace that fills our hearts with joy and love.

Just Do It

The only way to keep our hearts right before God is to exercise spiritually. We know what that means. We read and study our Bibles. We pray. We do good to those in need. We reflect and meditate on God. We know what it means to exercise spiritually. Do we do it? If not, chances are that it will catch up to us eventually, in the form of heart disease.

Our physical bodies may warn us of impending heart problems if we're fortunate; we may get a high cholesterol reading or even suffer a mild heart attack. Or... we might not. Sometimes, the first hint of heart trouble is sudden death. Do we want to take that chance?

It also works that way in our spiritual lives. We can go along for days, months, and years, spiritually drifting. We still go to church—at least most of the time. We still think we are Christians and would be shocked if someone told us otherwise. But when was the last time we read the Bible for ourselves, on our own time? How much time do we spend in prayer? When did we ever personally feed the hungry? Outside, we seem fine. Inside, our faith is shrinking.

I don't mean to imply that our spiritual health is based merely on externals. Every winter I have a problem with dry skin. My legs get so dry and itch so bad that I scratch them without realizing it. Sometimes they are so dry and I scratch so much that they bleed. I finally went to the doctor about my dry skin. Know what he did first? He didn't look at my legs. He didn't give me skin cream. The first thing he did was get out his stethoscope and listen to my heart. Why? I had dry skin, not a bad heart! But the doctor knew that the most superficial ailment might be a symptom of deeper trouble.

It's the same way spiritually. If we don't praise and give and study and pray as we should, our problem is more than skin deep. It's a heart problem. Yet our spiritual hearts are helped by exercise, just as our physical hearts are. Why don't we do our spiritual exercises? For the same reasons we don't exercise physically: it takes time and discipline; we get too busy, or too lazy, or too distracted.

If we fear sudden death by heart attack, should we not fear even more a hard heart that turns away from the living God? Can spiritual heart attacks strike as suddenly as physical ones? Can we think we're fine and, boom, we wake up one morning to find we've lost our faith?

It may seem that way, but such a loss does not happen overnight. Faith has to be strengthened each day by prayer, study, and service, or it will gradually die.

Is this a word of encouragement? Yes, because there is still time to find our way back to health. When it comes to physical exercise, the television ads urge us to "Just Do It." Spiritual exercise is the same. Encourage one another. Hold your faith until the end. Hear the voice of God in Jesus. Pray, study, and serve.

Just do it.

Questions for Discussion

1. Today, to be "hard-hearted" usually means to lack compassion. What does "hard-hearted" mean in Hebrews?

2. How is our situation today like Israel at the border of the Promised Land?

3. What are some ways in which sin is deceitful?

4. How can we spiritually encourage one another?

5. What are some spiritual exercises we need to practice to keep faith strong? Why is it so hard to practice them?

5
Trying to Get Some Rest

There remains, then, a Sabbath-rest for the people of God.
Hebrews 4:9

It's a typical day. The alarm rings, stirring you out of a peaceful slumber. Your first thought: "I wish I could go back to sleep."

But you can't. You wake up the kids and get them dressed. You shower, fix breakfast, pack lunches, kiss the kids good-bye, brave the cold, fight the traffic, and arrive at work ten minutes late. It's not even 8 a.m. and you're already exhausted.

The day continues with meetings, deadlines, interruptions, and phone calls. Finally, it's time to go home. You fix supper, drive Suzy to her basketball practice and Johnny to his piano lesson (on separate sides of town, of course), and arrive back at home to counsel your sister on the phone. Then back to get the kids and finally the nightly struggle of homework, teeth brushing, and tucking-in. You fall into bed yourself, exhausted.

Then the alarm rings and it starts all over.

Weary to the Bone

Sound familiar? If we could wish for anything in the world, wouldn't we wish for a minute or even a day to rest? To relax and unwind? We're overworked, and it seems no matter how hard we try we just can't seem to slow down.

Vacations don't seem to help. What's restful about a family vacation? When psychologists list the most stressful situations of modern life, "vacation" is near the top of the list. We plan the trip, spend more money than we should, and still come home more exhausted than when we left. We need a vacation to recover from the vacation.

Even a day or a week off doesn't help. Getting away by ourselves with absolutely no responsibilities doesn't help. The exhaustion we feel is too deep to be cured by a little rest. It's too deep for words. We are not just tired of our jobs, our friends, and even our families. We're tired of life itself.

That deep-seated weariness of life is well expressed by Paul Simon in his song, "American Tune":

Many's the time I've been mistaken,
and many times confused,
Yes, and I've often felt forsaken,
and certainly misused.

Oh, but I'm all right, I'm all right,
I'm just weary to my bones.
Still, you don't expect to be bright and bon
    vivant,
so far away from home,
so far away from home.

And I don't know a soul who's not been
    battered,
I don't have a friend who feels at ease,
I don't know a dream that's not been shattered
or driven to its knees...

But it's all right, it's all right,
you can't be forever blessed.
Still, tomorrow's going to be another working
   day,
and I'm trying to get some rest.
That's all, I'm trying to get some rest.

Surely that's what we're all trying to do. Just get some rest. The writer of Hebrews has an encouraging word to those who are tired. There is rest. Sweet rest from God. It's rest unlike any other we've ever known.

What does this rest look like?

The Joy of Salvation

The ultimate rest for God's people comes through Jesus. The writer of Hebrews compares Jesus to Joshua. This comparison would be more obvious to first century Christians because they knew "Jesus" and "Joshua" were two forms of the same name. Joshua led the children of Israel into the land of Canaan, the land of God's promised rest.

"Yeshua"

> So the Lord gave Israel all the land he had sworn to give to their forefathers, and they took possession of it and settled there. The Lord gave them rest on every side, just as he had sworn to their forefathers. Not one of their enemies withstood them; the Lord handed all their enemies over to them. Not one of the Lord's good promises to the house of Israel failed; every one was fulfilled.
>
> (Joshua 21:43-45)

Through Joshua, God gave Israel rest from their enemies. But it was not the ultimate rest God has in store for his people.

For if Joshua had given them rest, God would have not spoken later about another day. There remains, then, a Sabbath-rest for the people of God.

(Hebrews 4:8-9)

God gave Israel rest from their enemies through Joshua. He gives us rest from our enemies through Jesus. What are our greatest enemies? Sin, guilt, and death. "The last enemy to be destroyed is death" (1 Corinthians 15:26). How does Jesus give us rest from these enemies? By the cross and the empty tomb.

Perhaps you remember part of John Bunyan's classic allegory, *Pilgrim's Progress*. The main character of the story is named Christian. Christian lives in the City of Destruction. He goes about his business with a huge weight on his shoulders, a weight he cannot remove: the weight of sin, guilt, and death. Christian is directed by one named Evangelist to flee the City of Destruction by way of a narrow gate.

Christian enters the gate and goes up a narrow path to a hill. On the hill is a cross, and at the bottom of the hill is a tomb. As Christian approaches the cross, the burden falls off his back, rolls into the tomb, and is seen no more. Christian begins to sing and leap for joy. His sin is lifted, his burden gone. For the first time in his life, he's found rest and peace.

The rest God brings through Jesus is the rest of salvation. When we see what Jesus did for us at the cross, our hearts seem light, our burdens are lifted, and we shout with joy. In the middle of the busyness of life we find a calm the world cannot understand. Through Christ we rest secure with God. Sin and guilt no longer sap our energy. All our shattered dreams no longer matter for we have found our rest, our home with God.

The Rest That Comes Through Work

Rest and work are opposites. At least, that's the way we usually think. Even God rested from his work of creation.

> And yet his work has been finished since the creation of the world. For somewhere he has spoken about the seventh day in these words: "And on the seventh day God rested from all his work."
>
> (Hebrews 4:3-4)

Since the sixth day of creation, God has rested. Does that mean God has done no work since then? Of course not. God worked in the flood, in the call of Abraham, in the exodus, and in the exile. He worked through Jesus to save the world. His work continues in the world and in the church. He works in you and in me.

Strangely enough, then, the rest God has enjoyed since creation is the rest found in work. God's rest is just another name for his work, and to enter his rest is to become co-workers with him. We rest by working with God.

Jesus talks about this strange work that is really rest. To those who are exhausted and trying to get some rest, he says:

> Come to me, all you who are weary and burdened, and I will give you rest. Take my yoke upon you and learn from me, for I am gentle and humble in heart, and you will find rest for your souls. For my yoke is easy and my burden is light.
>
> (Matthew 11:29-30)

"I will give you rest—You will find rest for your souls."

That's exactly what we need to hear. The burdens of life, both great and small, are lifted by the hands of Jesus. Our weariness of soul disappears into his rest. We are at ease.

But then Jesus ruins it all by talking of a burden and a yoke. We're desperate to get rid of our burdens; why does he put another on us? Jesus wants to put a yoke on us—a heavy wooden collar placed on oxen so they can pull a plow! What kind of rest is this? It sounds like the worst of manual labor—the type of work we would do anything to avoid.

But this burden and yoke do not ruin our rest. They are our rest. They are the way we work with Jesus and he works with us. The yoke is a double yoke; it takes a pair of oxen to plow. When we place Jesus' yoke around our necks, he is there beside us, pulling with us and pulling for us. He takes the overwhelming load of sin off our backs and replaces it with another burden—one he helps us carry. The load of work that is really rest.

The yoke we wear is easy and the burden we carry is light because Jesus is in us. "It is Christ who lives in me" (Galatians 2:20). All the work we now do, we do for God. All the work we do for God, Christ does for us—in us. Paul tells us "to work out your own salvation with fear and trembling" (Philippians 2:12). That doesn't sound like rest. It sounds like bone-numbing work. But keep reading. "Work out your own salvation with fear and trembling, for it is God who works in you to will and to act according to his good purpose" (Philippians 2:12-13).

We work for God. We work hard: harder than we've ever worked—with fear and trembling.

Yet this work is actually the rest we long for. It's rest because God works in us. He inspires us with the will to work, inspires the work itself. Jesus bears the load and the Spirit produces the fruit.

Why do we worship God when we're exhausted?

Why do we help the needy when we really don't feel like it? Why do we continue to be good husbands and wives when the thrill is gone? Why struggle to be good parents when our kids give us grief? Why do our best at work when no one notices? Don't we get tired of it all? Don't we want to quit? Don't we just want some rest?

But we continue because Jesus is within us. He strengthens our will, gives us power, and lives in us. Any good we do, we accomplish not through our own power but through his. Christians are not naturally better than other people. We tire just as easily, and sometimes we even tire of doing good. But still we do what is right because we are not doing it anymore—Christ is. He lives in us. This is the secret of the easy yoke and the light burden. This is the work that is really rest.

How to Enter the Once-and-Future Rest

To be relieved of our burden of sin is truly rest. To work with Christ is to be at rest. Yet we look forward to the time when we lay our burdens down and go to be with God. Then we will enjoy complete rest.

The rest God promises is thus both present and future. It is a rest we have in the middle of our busy work-a-day lives. It is also the rest we will experience at the end of time.

> There remains, then, a Sabbath-rest for the people of God; for anyone who enters God's rest also rests from his own work, just as God did from his. Let us, therefore, make every effort to enter that rest, so that no one will fall by following their example of disobedience.

(Hebrews 4:9-11)

We rest eternally when we rest in God. That rest begins now as we do the work of God. If we trust God, we will rest in Christ at death. But the summit of God's rest will be reached only on the last day. The dead will be raised, those living in Christ will meet him in the air, "and so we will be with the Lord forever" (1 Thessalonians 4:17). To be with Christ forever: that alone is rest.

What must we do to enter that rest? The writer of Hebrews says it takes effort. "Let us, therefore, make every effort to enter that rest" (Hebrews 4:11). Finding rest is hard work! But that doesn't mean we earn God's rest; this is not a call to legalism. Instead, the effort we make is the effort of faith. "Now we who have believed enter that rest..." (Hebrews 4:3).

God promises rest: more restful than the longest vacation, than retirement, than the laziest day you've ever known—eternal rest.

Do you trust God's promise? That's the faith we are called to, the faith that God will deliver his rest. That faith demands more than mere agreement; it demands obedience. God promised Israel they would rest in the promised land. They did not believe his promise and so they "did not go in, because of disobedience" (Hebrews 4:6). We grasp God's promise through faithful, daily obedience. He conquers every foe we face, any enemy that keeps us from his rest.

Hang in There, Rest is Coming

So, no matter how tiring life gets, we put our trust in Jesus. That trust removes our load of sin, giving us rest from the burden of guilt. That trust transforms the daily grind into work done for Jesus—work that is really rest. That trust assures us that at our death we will rest forever in him.

Are you tired? Bone tired? Harried? Hassled?

Weary? Don't give up. Rest is coming—the only rest that truly satisfies.

There was once a man who could find no rest. He tried to find it in pleasure; he searched for it in accomplishment. Still he found himself burdened with a restless heart. Finally, he came to faith in Jesus. Reflecting on the shape of his early life, this man, Augustine, prayed this way on the first page of his Confessions: "Oh Lord, you have made us for Yourself, and our hearts are restless until we rest in You."

The next time the kids are loud, traffic is heavy, the deadline looms, and there aren't enough minutes in the day, ask yourself this question: "Would you like to get some rest?"

Trust Jesus. Rest in him now—and forever.

Questions for Discussion

1. What are some ways we try to find rest? Do they work?

2. What spiritual enemies have we triumphed over in Christ?

3. How can work be rest? How can God rest on the seventh day and still continue to work?

4. How do you picture heaven as rest?

5. Does it take effort to enter God's rest? How can that be?

6
Help!

Let us then approach the throne of grace with confidence,
so that we may receive mercy and find grace to help us in
our time of need.

Hebrews 4:16

I'll never forget my shortest, most sincere prayer. It was many years ago, when I lived in Memphis. One drizzly day, I was driving through the winding streets downtown. As I came around a corner, I noticed the car in front of me was going very slowly. Suddenly, I noticed it wasn't going at all.

I hit my brakes and began to slide—sideways, at forty miles an hour. The stalled car's rear bumper rushed up to meet me. It all happened so quickly, but at the time it seemed as if the moments dragged by. I distinctly remember thinking, "This is it. I'm going to die."

At that point I prayed my shortest, most sincere prayer: "Help!"

And God heard my prayer. Oh, I hit the car in front of me, all right, but no one was in it and I escaped without a scratch. After bending my fender back into shape, I could even drive my car. The Lord heard and protected.

I've thought often about that prayer and prayed it several times since then. "Help!" It's the most basic of prayers, yet the most heart-felt. Not just in the crises of life, but in the day-to-day grind as well, we need help.

Could you use some help? The encouraging word of Hebrews is that Jesus is there to help us.

Help With Our Weaknesses

At times we all feel weak and helpless. We need someone to give us strength—strength against temptation, strength to love those around us, sometimes, even, strength to get out of bed and start the day.

What kind of person do we need to help us when we're weak? We need someone who is strong—at least, stronger than we are. It does no good to cry for help if those who hear us are as helpless as we. We need a rescuer.

You've seen the old Tarzan movies. Remember how at least once in every movie, someone falls in the quicksand and begins to sink? Have you ever fallen in the quicksand of life? Perhaps you're there now, sinking slowly into the cares and pressures that drag you down. No matter how much you struggle, it only makes things worse. Finally, in desperation, you cry out, "Help!"

Who do you want to come to save you? Do you want someone who'll sympathize? "I know just how you feel," this person might say. "I was in the quicksand once, myself. You're beginning to panic now aren't you? The sand is past your chin, your heart is pounding, and you're thrashing uncontrollably. Oh yes, I remember it well."

Sympathy is all well and good, but when we're sinking in quicksand what we need most is someone with a stout arm, standing on solid ground. We need someone strong, someone with the power to help.

Jesus is that someone. He pulls us from the sinking sands of despair with his powerful hand. He can help because he stands on the firm ground of heaven.

Therefore, since we have a great high priest who has gone through the heavens, Jesus the Son of God, let us hold firmly to the faith we possess.

(Hebrews 4:14)

No matter how helpless our situation, Jesus has the power to save. He is the Almighty Son of God who throws us a rope from heaven: the rope of faith. All we must do is hold firmly to that faith while he pulls us from the sands of trouble.

Who do we want to help us in trouble? Someone who has the power, someone who can. But we also want someone with gentleness and sympathy. When you're in the quicksand you can't be picky, but if possible I'd rather have a sympathetic rescuer. When we're caught up in our troubles, we don't need someone who will scold and say, "How did you get in such a mess? How stupid can you be? If you'd stuck to the path, you'd never fallen into this stuff."

We know we're stupid; we don't need to be reminded. We need help: caring, gentle, sympathetic help.

Think of a doctor. When we're sick, what kind of doctor do we want? First of all, we want a doctor who can cure us; we don't want a doctor who's sicker than we are. At least, we don't want one who is so sick he can't cure us. On the other hand, would we want a doctor who'd never been sick a day in his life? I don't think so. We'd want one who knows what it's like to be sick, in pain, and afraid: a doctor who cares, feels, and sympathizes.

That's the way of the great physician. He can help us because he's strong and able. But he also helps with gentleness, because he is human, too. He knows what it's like to be in pain.

> For we do not have a high priest who is unable to sympathize with our weaknesses, but we have one who has been tempted in every way, just as we are—yet was without sin.

(Hebrews 4:15)

Jesus is the great high priest who has passed through the heavens. He has the power to help. He also is one who knows what it's like to need help. He was tempted and tried just as we are. Think about that—just as we are. He knows what it's like to sink beneath the troubles of life. He faced betrayal, abandonment, and pain. At times he wanted to take the wrong path and make the wrong choice, but he didn't. Why? Because he cried out for help.

> During the days of Jesus' life on earth, he offered up prayers and petitions with loud cries and tears to the one who could save him from death, and he was heard because of his reverent submission.

> (Hebrews 5:7)

Jesus knows what it's like to be tempted, weak, and helpless. "He is able to deal gently with those who are ignorant and going astray, since he himself is subject to weakness" (Hebrews 5:2). When tempted, Jesus cried out to God for help. God heard and helped. In the garden, Jesus cried, "My Father, if it is possible, may this cup be taken from me. Yet not as I will, but as you will" (Matthew 26:39). He cried with tears and his sweat was as blood. At the weakest point of his life, on the cross, Jesus cried out to his Father, "My God, my God, why have you forsaken me?" (Mark 15:34). The writer of Hebrews says Jesus was heard by God, the one who could save him from death.

How? How did God answer Jesus' prayers to be saved from death? Did he save him from the cross? No. So, how was Jesus answered?

Jesus made another cry from the cross, his final cry: "Father, into your hands I commit my spirit" (Luke 23:46). God heard that cry and rescued Jesus from death by means of the resurrection.

Jesus knows what it's like to be at the end of the rope. He knows temptation, pain, stress, and even death. He overcame them all. Now at God's right hand, he has the power to help us, no matter what we face. And he helps with a gentle hand. He's been there, done that. Jesus: power and sympathy.

Help With Our Sins

Many times the particular weakness we face is temptation. "Sin" has become an outmoded word in our society. Most people don't speak of sin, except perhaps at church. Instead we prefer terms like "maladjustment," "bad judgment," or "error." Politicians are particularly adept at avoiding the term, preferring what is called the "culpable passive," as in, "Mistakes were made." We don't like "sin" because it smacks too much of church. It calls to mind the insincere tears of unscrupulous television preachers who parade their repentance before thousands.

The problem is, there's no better word for describing what we all have done. We've done more than goof or make mistakes. We have sinned. Perhaps it's time for the word "sin" to make a comeback. More than twenty years ago, the psychologist Karl Menninger wrote a book entitled *Whatever Became of Sin?* More recently, popular news magazines have bemoaned our culture's lack of shame and guilt. There was once a time when we would hide our shameful acts. Now we parade them on television talk shows.

All of us know, deep down, that there are things we have done that we do not want anyone to know about. We are ashamed and guilty. We have sinned and hurt others. We have offended the holy God. We need help with sin. We've already seen how Jesus helps us when we're tempted, but what happens when we give in to the temptation? Who can pull us from the quicksand of sin?

We know the answer: Jesus saves. He is our great high priest. What does a high priest do?

Every high priest is selected from among men and is appointed to represent them in matters related to God, to offer gifts and sacrifices for sin...

[A]nd having been made perfect, he [the Son] became the source of eternal salvation for all who obey him, having been designated by God a high priest according to the order of Melchizidek.

(Hebrews 5:1, 9)

Jesus offered a sacrifice for our sins; that's what high priests do. But Jesus did more than that. He offered himself on the cross as a sacrifice for our sins. He is both priest and sacrifice. Because he died for us, we no longer have to worry about sin. All our sins—past, present, and future—are nailed to the cross. We ask for help against sin and get it, because Jesus paid it all.

Help With Obedience

Jesus forgives our sins once and for all. Out of love and gratitude, we follow him. We pledge to be his disciples, to go wherever he goes. We don't always live up to that pledge. We need help with obedience.

Obedience is another out-of-date word. At least, some think so. We prefer freedom to obedience. We want to be our masters, make our own decisions. We desire to hold our own destiny in our hands. We want to be the boss. And yet, we aren't. We are truly free only when we obey the one who made us, who died for us, who is our brother.

But obedience does not come easy—at least it never has for me. I was a good kid, one who seldom got in trouble and almost always did what my parents wanted... unless I wanted something else.

I distinctly remember the day my dad taught me what obedience is all about. He said, "Obeying your parents means doing what they say even when you don't want to do it!" That seems so obvious, but it's not. It works the same way with God. We go day after day, thinking we are good, obedient Christians. In fact, we are just doing what we want to. It just so happens that what we want to do is what God wants us to do.

One day that changes. We bump up against a command from God that makes us very uncomfortable. "Go sell all you have and give to the poor." "Deny yourself and take up the cross." "Wash one another's feet." "Love your enemies."

The list could go on and on. When we face those uncomfortable passages, we can explain them away, ignore them, or try to justify our failure to follow them. But that's not obedience.

To obey is to do the will of God, especially when we find it hard. G.K. Chesterton once said, "Christianity has not been tried and found wanting. It's been found difficult and left untried." How do we obey when it's difficult? How do we obey when we don't want to?

We need help. Obedience is learned through pain and suffering; even Jesus had to learn it that way.

> Although he was a son, he learned obedience from what he suffered and, once made perfect, he became the source of eternal salvation for all who obey him and was designated by God to be high priest in the order of Melchizedek.

> (Hebrews 5:8-10)

Jesus learned obedience. He was made perfect. What can this mean? I thought Jesus was perfect, the sinless Son of God. We understand how we must learn obedience, but how did Jesus have to learn it?

The word "perfect" here is better translated "complete." Jesus was sinless, but he was not the complete Savior until he became one of us. He suffered temptation. At least part of him, if only for a moment, did not want to do what God commanded. Isn't that what temptation means? At least part of Jesus did not want to go to the cross. He wanted the cup to pass. He wanted it so much that he sweated <u>blood</u>. *Luke 22:44 "like"*

But he learned to obey, to do what the Father wanted, even if it wasn't what he wanted. "Let this cup pass," he prayed. "Yet not my will, but yours." More than anything else, Jesus wanted to do the will of the Father.

Isn't that obedience? Isn't that what we need to learn? We need to learn to put our deepest desires behind the greatest desire of all: the desire to do the will of God, to obey.

We need help with obedience, and Jesus gives us that help. His power not only forgives all our sins, it also gives us the will to obey. He is the source of salvation, the source of obedience.

Salvation Means Being Helped

Bill stands in front of a group of strangers. All eyes are on him. His palms are clammy, his knees weak. He's about to do the hardest thing he's ever done in his life. He begins in a croaking voice, "My name is Bill." He pauses and swallows. "And I'm an alcoholic." The first step toward sobriety is admitting he needs help. It's also the first step toward God.

"Jesus saves," we say. We often talk and sing of salvation. Why is it that so many reject the salvation Jesus brings? Perhaps part of the reason is the very word "salvation." The word looks too much like stained glass, smells too much like musty church buildings, and reminds us too much of pinched-faced religious people.

But what is salvation? Being helped, that's all. Maybe we'd get more to accept the message if we put it that way. Perhaps we should place "Jesus Helps" on our church signs, billboards, and tee shirts. To be saved is to admit that we need the help of Jesus: help with our weakness, our sins, our obedience.

Jesus hears our cry for help. Our cry of weakness soon becomes a cry of confidence.

Let us then approach the throne of grace with confidence, so that we may receive mercy and find grace to help us in our time of need.

(Hebrews 4:16)

Salvation means being helped. That may seem obvious. But how often do we try to live life on our own power? How often do we try to overcome our sins and faults by ourselves? How often do we think we can obey if we just try a little harder? Too often. But in our saner moments we remember the lesson we learned as a child. The lesson from the first hymn most of us learned.

Jesus loves me, this I know
for the Bible tells me so.

Little ones to him belong,
they are weak, but he is strong.

Perhaps this is what Jesus meant when he said, "I tell you the truth, anyone who will not receive the kingdom of God like a little child will never enter it" (Luke 18:17). Children know they are little ones, that they are weak. Adults sometimes forget. But we are children, too. We need someone to help us.

We are weak and cry for help; he is strong. He hears and gives us strength.

Jesus loves me. Yes, indeed.

Questions for Discussion

1. Give some examples of when you prayed for help.

2. How does it help us to know that Jesus also prayed for help?

3. Do you find it hard to obey? Why? Does our culture emphasize the value of obedience? Why or why not?

4. Jesus was perfect. Why did he need to learn obedience?

5. What makes us think God will hear us when we ask for help?

7
To The Very End

We want each of you to show this same diligence to the very end, in order to make your hope sure.

Hebrews 6:11

I write this on the last day of January, which means it's about time to look at how I've done with my New Year's resolutions. The answer is... not very well.

I don't think I'm alone. Many of us make New Year's resolutions. Mine are usually the same each year: eat less, exercise more, sin less, pray more. I always make a good start on my resolutions; it's easy to start. But by the end of January—sometimes even sooner—I find that I've done in the new year pretty much what I did in the old one. It's easier to start than to finish.

That's true in all of life. We start improvements around the house, fully intending to finish them, but we never quite get around to it. We plan to fix the leaking faucet someday. We even bought the tools to do it. We'll start tomorrow. Meanwhile, dresses are half-sewn, letters partially written, and half-done projects litter the garage. The clean dishes sit in the dishwasher; we'll put them away later.

Finishing is harder than starting. It happens in the most important parts of life. Businesses start with a boom and then go bankrupt. Every marriage begins in hope, but many end with failure.

It's not how you start, it's how you finish. Sometimes you even start, quit, and cannot get started again.

Will We Fall Away?

It happens in our spiritual lives, too. We begin our walk with Christ full of great excitement. We fully intend to follow him wherever he leads. We are in for the duration; we'll follow all the way.

But after a while, Christianity becomes too daily. It's the same thing, over and over again: The same sins, the same repentance, the same prayers, the same worship, the same old Bible stories. We want to follow Jesus, but we begin to drift. We are distracted. Our excitement cools, our dedication weakens. We begin to neglect prayer and study and church. Before we know it, our faith is weak, perhaps even dead.

What then?

We can come to our senses and turn back to God. He is always there with open arms to welcome us home, no matter how prodigal we are, no matter how far we've roamed.

But the cycle can begin again. We drift... our excitement cools... faith grows weak. Still the Father waits for us to return. But what if we can't? What if we won't? If we refuse to finish, to turn back to God, what fate awaits us?

In one of the strongest warnings in the Bible, the writer of Hebrews tells what can happen to those who start and do not finish:

> It is impossible for those who have once been enlightened, who have tasted the heavenly gift, who have shared in the Holy Spirit, who have tasted the goodness of the word of God and the powers of the coming age, if they fall away, to be brought back to repentance, because to their loss they are crucifying the Son of God all over again and subjecting him to public disgrace.

(Hebrews 6:4-6)

"It's impossible to bring them back." These are some of the scariest words in the Bible. It's frightening to think there are people who cannot be brought back to God. It's even more frightening to think we are among them.

A few days ago a deeply troubled young man came to talk with me. He thought he had committed an unpardonable sin. "Does God add up all our sins?" he asked. You see, he had been raised as a Christian, then he'd turned his back on the Lord. In his own words, he had committed "some of the big sins" in that time. Recently he had returned to the Lord and his church. "But even now," he said, "I have terrible, blasphemous thoughts come in my mind, thoughts I cannot control. Is there any hope for me?"

What would you have told him? Is there hope for him or is it impossible for him to come back?

I told him God's grace was bigger than all his sins—bigger than all your sins or my sins. Bigger than all the sins since Adam. Why did I tell him this? Because the Bible says, "But where sin increased, grace increased all the more..." (Romans 5:20). You can't out-sin the grace of God.

But if that's true, why does the writer of Hebrews say these people cannot be brought back to repentance? Is their sin too great for God's grace? No. God's grace covers any and all sin. But God does not force his grace upon us. Grace must be received in faith. And although it seems unbelievable, there are some who will not turn back to God and receive his grace.

Who are these people who will not turn back to God? First, they are those who once were completely Christian. They had been enlightened. They knew Jesus, "the true light that gives light to every man" (John 1:9). They had tasted the heavenly gift of salvation, "tasted that the Lord is good" (1 Peter 2:3). They had shared in the Holy Spirit, the gift they had received at baptism (Acts

2:38). They had tasted the goodness of God's word and the power of the kingdom.

Enlightened, tasted, shared... All words of experience. These people had a genuine experience of God. They did not simply appear to be saved, they were saved—fully and completely—by the grace of God. Father, Son, and Spirit made their home in them.

Then, the unthinkable happened: they evicted God. They threw him out of their lives by refusing to grow spiritually. That refusal was not once upon a time, but continuous. "They are crucifying the Son of God all over again and subjecting him to public disgrace."

Imagine... crucifying Jesus: driving nails in his flesh and a spear in his side, mocking him as he bleeds out his life. Once these people experienced the goodness of Jesus. Now they stab him, not in the back, but publicly, for all the world to see.

It's impossible to save such people, impossible even for God.

"How can that be?" you ask. "Can't God do everything?"

No. He can't give us free will and then force us to follow him. He can only draw us by his grace and love.

The writer of Hebrews gives an illustration (6:7-8). Like land that drinks in the rain, these people had received the blessings of God through Christ. But instead of producing a good crop for God, they had repaid his blessings with thorns and thistles. They continue to throw God's blessings back in his face. They will not turn back to God.

Do you want to turn back to God but think you're too far gone? Turn anyway, just a little. Make even the smallest move toward God and he will meet you with open arms. No sin is too big or too horrible for him to forgive. The blood of Christ covers them all.

But be warned: we can slip so far away from God that we do not want to return. We cannot repent because we refuse to repent. Jesus' blood covers all sin, but we can't come to the cross if we continue to nail Jesus onto it. No power on earth and heaven, not even the overwhelming power of God's love, can move us if we stubbornly refuse to be moved.

A child falls down a well. She calls for help. Rescuers come and crowd around the mouth of the well. They toss the girl a rope. Out of fear or spite she will not grab the rope.

What can you do?

A rescuer risks his life by being lowered into the well. He grabs the little girl who's kicking and screaming. Slowly, they both are pulled up the dank, dark well.

Halfway up the girl wrenches herself free and plummets back to the darkness below.

God came all the way down into the well to rescue us. He became one of us. Jesus grabbed us and hauled us out of sin, kicking and screaming. But if we continue to refuse his help, if we plummet again to the depths of sin, if we will not grasp the hand he gives us, then as much as it breaks his heart, he cannot save. He cannot turn those who will not be turned. It's impossible.

Better Things

Will we fall away from Christ? Will we refuse to return?

Of course not!

Even though we speak like this, dear friends, we are confident of better things in your case—things that accompany salvation.

(Hebrews 6:9)

When I was a college student I had a fairly heated discussion with one of my professors. He argued that not only was it possible to fall from God's grace but it was probable. More than likely, he said, we all will fall. I believed then (and even more so now) that the professor ignored the clear teaching of the Bible on the assurance of salvation. We don't have to guess if we are right with God, we can know we are through faith.

I didn't know it then, but the writer of Hebrews is on my side. Even after giving the strongest warning in the Bible against falling away from God, he says, "For you, falling is possible, but not probable. We expect better things from you."

The point is that our walk with God should be a consistent one. We should grow in faith, knowing that the alternative to growth is not stability, but stagnation and death. The Hebrews had stagnated in their spiritual growth.

> In fact, though by this time you ought to be teachers, you need someone to teach you the elementary truths of God's word all over again. You need milk, not solid food!

> (Hebrews 5:12)

They had failed to grow as they should. They had neglected God's word. They should be sharing that word with others but instead needed a refresher course themselves. They were slipping, in danger of falling away from God.

But the writer of Hebrews knew these people; he believed in them. He knew the way they had begun their walk of service. He had confidence in their willingness to turn back to God.

More importantly, he knew the God they served. God the Father does not delight in watching his children fall. He is no ogre waiting to punish and devour those who stray from the path. No, he is a loving Father who waits to receive them back with open arms. He is a faithful God who remembers when his children were loving and obedient.

> God is not unjust; he will not forget your work and the love you have shown him as you helped his people and continue to help them.
>
> (Hebrews 6:10)

Here our service to God is measured by our continued service to others. We will not fall away from him if we stay close to one another. We are to feed on God's word—on meat, not milk. But spiritual growth is measured not just in how much Scripture we know, but how much we practice. We know God's will by doing God's will. His will is for us to feed the hungry, clothe the naked, heal the sick, and bring them the good news of Jesus. Few on earth may know the good work we do, but God will know.

We don't doubt that God remembers the work of famous heroes of the faith: healers, missionaries, and martyrs. Everyone's heard of Billy Graham and Mother Teresa. But what about the work of ordinary Christians like us?

One of my unsung heroes of the faith is my wife's Aunt Mabel who spent her life caring for others. She and Uncle Frank took into their home uncounted foster children and cared for them as their own. Mabel nursed her own parents until their death. She cared for her bed-ridden father-in-law and mother-in-law, both with Alzheimer's, until they passed away. She did detestable tasks with a smile on her face and a willing heart. She worked so hard for others that her willing heart finally gave out; Mabel died young. Few know how much she gave of herself; few remember.

My parents are heroes, too. For years, my mother cared for her sister Ruth, who suffered from multiple sclerosis and was confined to a nursing home. Ruth was a difficult, unappreciative patient, but that did not diminish my mother's care and loyalty. Now, with the same patience and gentleness, Mom cares for her father. At different times my dad has taken care of his mother-in-law, his father-in-law, his mother, and his father. Those of you who are caregivers to the elderly know the strains and challenges he faces. Few appreciate what Mom and Dad do. Still, they faithfully care for their family.

In George Eliot's *Middlemarch*, the main character, Dorothea, is a woman who spends her whole life in service to others. Much of that service is done quietly and anonymously. Almost all goes unnoticed. That is the way of all true service. In Eliot's words:

> Her full nature... spent itself in channels which had no great name on earth. But the effect of her being on those around her was incalculably diffuse: for the growing good of the world is partly dependent on unhistoric acts; and that things are not so ill with you and me as they might have been, is half owing to the number who lived faithfully a hidden life, and rest in unvisited tombs.

Mabel... Dorothea... Mom... Dad... Others are not remembered. Will we be remembered when we are dead and gone?

Surely, By some and for a while. But life will go on without us, memories will fade, and soon no one will remember our loving acts of service. No one will remember our names, our unhistoric acts, our hidden lives.

No one but God. And that is enough-enough to keep us loyal to the God who is loyal to us.

Keep On To the End

There are two ways: the way of neglect that leads to spiritual immaturity, falling away from God, and crucifying Christ afresh; or the way of growth that leads to solid spiritual food, service to others, and being remembered by God. All who are Christians have started down the second path of obedience. The question is: will we continue?

What does it take to continue on the path to God? Faith, patience, diligence.

> We want each of you to show this same diligence to the very end, in order to make your hope sure. We do not want you to become lazy, but to imitate those who through faith and patience inherit what has been promised.

> (Hebrews 6:11-12)

"It's impossible to bring them back to repentance." Those chilling words began this section of Hebrews. Do they mean we must live each moment in danger of falling away from God?

No. Hebrews is a word of encouragement. The encouraging word here is that we can be sure of our hope. How can we be sure? By continuing our service to others, by showing diligence in our walk with God, and by continuing to trust Jesus for salvation until the very end.

We walk with God. We run the path of growth and service. That walk, that run, is not a sprint but a marathon. No matter how our feet hurt and our lungs ache, we must continue to the finish. Paul says, "I have finished the race" (2 Timothy 4:7). He's not the only one. There are countless others who have finished before us, who have won the victory through faith and patience. It's not how you start, it's how you finish. We must finish, too.

And so we will, by God's grace. We will if we don't become lazy and complacent.

How's your walk with God, your run with Jesus? Did you begin well and then begin to tire? Have you taken your eye off the goal? Have you slowed or even stopped in your spiritual growth? Do you serve those in need as you once did?

If you've stopped on the path, it's not too late to start again. Assurance of victory can be yours, can be ours—but only if we shake off our sluggishness and turn back to God. He waits, calls, and cheers us on. He reaches out his arms to help.

We dare not refuse those loving arms.

Questions for Discussion

1. What are some resolutions you made and did not keep or projects you have begun and not finished?

2. Is there a place for frightening people into obeying God? Is this what Hebrews 6:4-6 is trying to do?

3. What would you tell people who think they've sinned so horribly that they can't come back to God? Since Hebrew tells certain people it is impossible to repent, should we tell certain people the same thing?

4. Is it probable we will fall from grace? Is it possible?

5. Is failure to grow as a Christian the same as crucifying Christ afresh?

6. Who are some of the "unsung heroes" of the faith in your life?

8
Renegotiating the Contract

The time is coming, declares the Lord, when I will make a new covenant...

Hebrews 8:8

It's a familiar story in the sports section: a ballplayer has a great year, maybe even a career year. Although he already makes millions, he and his agent have a bright idea—renegotiating his contract. They approach the owner and negotiations commence. Out of fear of losing the great player and the fan support he generates, the owner finally caves in, making the millionaire player a multi-millionaire.

Renegotiating the contract. It sounds like nothing but greed when millions are involved. But wouldn't we all like to renegotiate our contracts? Wouldn't it be great to get a better contract at work, a fresh start in our families, or a new deal in life?

Imagine... The boss comes in and says, "Billy, you've been doing such a good job lately that I thought it only fair to increase your salary, benefits, and vacation time." Or your husband arrives home and announces, "Sally, I've been thinking lately about our family and it occurs to me that you've been pulling more than your share of the load. Why don't you take it easy this weekend and I'll watch the kids." Or your teenage son says, "Dad, now that I have a part-time job, I want to pay for the gas in the family car."

Sound far-fetched? Perhaps. But we can dream, can't we? No matter how sweet life is for us, we always long for more—a new contract, a better deal. Sometimes life's not so sweet. What we wouldn't sometimes give for a new deal on the job, at home, in all the business of life. But life is more and more of the same old thing. It never really changes, does it? It doesn't even seem possible for it to change.

If we're honest, we might even admit that we sometimes long for a new deal in our spiritual lives. We long for new spiritual life; we search for it in the latest Christian seminar, tape, or book. These resources seem to help for a while, but then our walk with Christ sinks into a routine. We hunger for a new start, a new deal with God.

The encouraging word from Hebrews is that God understands our desire for a new deal. He does more than understand; he gives us a new deal, the sweetest contract ever written.

The Old Deal

God led the Israelites from Egypt. His presence overshadowed Mount Sinai in fire and smoke. There, he made a deal with Israel. If they would keep his commandments and serve only him, then he would be their God and bless them. God said, "Now if you obey me fully and keep my covenant, then out of all the nations you will be my treasured possession" (Exodus 19:5).

The deal God made with Israel was called a covenant. Today we rarely speak of covenants outside of church. Instead we have deals and contracts. Unfortunately we've come to believe that deals are made to be broken and contracts always have fine print that allows one to get out of them. "Covenant" is a much more serious word than "deal" or "contract." This particular covenant was as sure as the word of God himself. God made a deal with Israel that he would never break.

Unfortunately, Israel broke the covenant through sin, by turning from God to idols. But God knew Israel was weak and made provision for forgiveness in his covenant. The Israelites could be forgiven if they brought sacrifices for the priests to offer to God. Through sacrifice, the covenant was repaired. The sacrificial system of the old covenant was a sign of God's mercy. It was how he forgave their sins. However, the sacrificial system had its limitations. Sacrifices had to be made continually. Priests were born, died, and new priests took their place. Forgiveness under this old deal was real but not permanent. When one sinned again, it was back to the priest with a sacrifice, again, and again, and again.

The old covenant was an amazing blessing from God, a great deal for Israel—but a limited deal. Its priests were human, its sacrifices repetitive, its temple merely a shadow of a heavenly sanctuary (Hebrews 8:5). In short, it was a faulty deal, because people are faulty. We sin, we need forgiveness, and we need a permanent solution to our sins. The fault is not in God, but in people.

> For if there had been nothing wrong with that first covenant, no place would have been sought for another. But God found fault with the people...
>
> (Hebrews 8:7-8)

The old covenant promised God's blessing to those who obeyed. But that's the problem: we humans don't always obey. It promised forgiveness to those who sacrificed, but sacrifices had to be made continually. What we need is a better deal, a permanent sacrifice.

The New Deal

Even back in Old Testament times, God promised his people a new and better deal. He promised it, even though his people didn't deserve it. In spite of his love for them, they turned from God to idols. They neglected the poor and needy. They relied on their status as God's nation instead of turning their hearts to God. Because of their disobedience, God announced through Jeremiah that he would send them into exile, not just to punish them, but to move them to repentance.

Jeremiah is usually called the weeping prophet because his message was one of destruction and judgment. Yet this same Jeremiah also has a word of grace and encouragement for his day and ours, a word quoted by Hebrews:

> The time is coming, declares the Lord, when I will make a new covenant with the house of Israel.... This is the covenant I will make with the house of Israel after that time, declares the Lord. I will put my laws in their minds and write them on their hearts. I will be their God, and they will be my people. No longer will a man teach his neighbor, or a man his brother, saying "Know the Lord," because they will all know me, from the least of them to the greatest. For I will forgive their wickedness and remember their sins no more.

> (Hebrews 8:8, 10-12)

God promised a new deal to Israel. That promise came true in Jesus. That new deal is not just for Jews but for all who come to God in faith. We don't deserve this new deal. It comes solely by the grace of God. What makes this new deal better than the old one?

First, it is better because God writes his laws on our minds and hearts. The old law, given on Mount Sinai, was never meant to be simply an external set of rules. Israel also should have obeyed God from the heart. But as we have already seen in Hebrews, their hearts were hardened by unbelief. As Paul puts it in Romans, the problem is not with the law but with us. "So then, the law is holy, and the commandment is holy, righteous, and good.... We know that the law is spiritual, but I am unspiritual..." (Romans 7:12, 14).

Under the old covenant, the law is good but people are powerless to keep it. What changes under the new covenant? How is it a better deal? God's law is still the same—holy, righteous, and good. But now God gives us the power to keep his law. His Holy Spirit lives in us, producing the fruit of righteous living. "For the law of the Spirit of life in Christ Jesus has set you free from the law of sin and death" (Romans 8:2, NRSV). In the words of Hebrews, the law now is in our minds and hearts. We keep God's law because God lives within us. He is our God, and we are his people.

The second reason this is a better deal is that all who are part of this new covenant "know the Lord." That sounds strange. "Of course they know the Lord," you think. "How can one be a part of God's covenant without knowing him?" Yet that's exactly what happened under the old covenant. One was born into that old covenant. Jewish babies knew no more about God than other babies, but they were part of God's covenant people. They enjoyed the covenant but had to be taught what it meant to know God. By contrast, one enters the new covenant not by birth, but by faith. One must know the Lord to be born again. Only those who know the Lord through faith enjoy the blessings of this new deal.

Of course, we should grow in our knowledge of the Lord. The new deal also promises a more intimate knowledge of God. He is our God, we are his people, and he lives within us by his Spirit. Thus, while those under the old covenant had a genuine experience of God, our experience of God is deeper and richer than the experience of those under the old covenant. We all know God and want to know him more.

Most importantly, the new deal is better because it provides a permanent forgiveness of sins. As we saw above, under the old deal the people had to bring sacrifice after sacrifice. Under the old covenant there was a long succession of high priests. No high priest could offer the ultimate sacrifice. Now there is a high priest who can—who did. Under the new deal, Jesus gave himself as a sacrifice for us, once-for-all.

> [B]ecause Jesus lives forever, he has a permanent priesthood. Therefore he is able to save completely those who come to God through him, because he always lives to intercede for them.
>
> Such a high priest meets our need—one who is holy, blameless, pure, set apart from sinners, exalted above the heavens. Unlike other high priest, he does not need to offer sacrifices day after day, first for his own sins, then for the sins of the people. He sacrificed himself for their sins once for all when he offered himself.
>
> (Hebrews 7:24-27)

We'll look more closely at the once-for-allness of our salvation in the next chapter. Here, the point is the superiority of the new deal God offers us. What do we need the most? Not a new deal at work or at home, but a new deal with God. We need someone—someone who takes away our sins, someone who gives us the power to fight sin, someone holy, someone pure, someone to make us holy and pure.

His name is Jesus. He is the ever-living high priest. He is the final sacrifice. He is the new deal God gives us, the new covenant. He is superior to all who went before him, and through him God's law is in our hearts. Through him we know God as we never did before. Through him we have forgiveness of sins. Through him we are saved completely.

What a deal!

Don't Look Back

Why does the writer of Hebrews spend so much time trying to convince his readers that the new covenant is superior to the old one? Isn't it obvious?

The answer is: it should have been obvious, but wasn't to some. It's likely that some of the readers of Hebrews were thinking of returning to that old deal. Why? Why return to what is inferior?

Because it's familiar. We always like what's familiar, even if the new is better. Have you ever gotten a new computer system? The new system promises to do so much more than the old. It lessens our workload, decreases paperwork, and runs five times faster than the old system... and we hate it. We hate it because it is new and unfamiliar. We long for the old.

We, who live many years after this letter was written, may think we feel no temptation to return to the old covenant. Or do we? Do we sometimes feel more comfortable with things the way they used to be? Do we still live as if we were under the old deal?

Are we ever tempted to be legalists, to base our salvation on our ability to be right? Some are. Maybe all of us are at times, if we're honest with ourselves. Some of us still cannot break away from the idea that the law of God is a list of external rules we must obey, that being right with God is a matter of being right on certain religious issues. Which issues, you ask? It depends on whom you ask. At times we still are not convinced that the law is in our hearts and minds, that Jesus lives within us through his Spirit, or that he keeps the law for us.

What about priests? The old deal was weak because it demanded that one go to a succession of human priests for salvation. Today we reject the idea of priests who stand between us and God. We know the Bible teaches the priesthood of all believers, so no priests for us, thank you very much.

But what about preachers? Are we not tempted, at times, to place our trust in human leaders of the church? The celebrity in the pulpit, the best-selling author, or the effective counselor can each become the one we trust to give us the answers to our spiritual quandaries. We know better; we know that spiritual leaders have fallen in the past and will again. We know we've been burned before by trusting too much in the wisdom of the well-known. Still, we sometimes make our leaders more than they should be.

We are also strangely drawn to the temporary forgiveness under the old covenant. No, we aren't likely to start sacrificing animals for our sins. But at times we do feel that our sins are so great and so numerous that they can't be forgiven. I talked with a woman this week who was raised in the church. "I never stopped believing the whole thing," she told me. But she had drifted away from the Lord for years. Now she wanted to return but wasn't sure God would accept her. "I've sinned so much for so long."

Hebrews says Jesus died once for all sin—past, present, and future. Jesus is our great High Priest, he and no other. We need no human being to give us the answers and bring us to God. Jesus does that—Jesus alone. Through Jesus and the Spirit, God has written his law on our hearts. Now we want to obey him, not in order to be saved, but because we are saved.

His law in our hearts... A perfect Priest... Full forgiveness: That's the deal God offers, the best deal anywhere.

Don't look back. Sign the deal.

Questions for Discussion

1. What are some "new deals" in life you would make for yourself if you could?

2. In what ways was the old covenant a blessing from God? What were its limitations?

3. What does it mean to have God's laws written on our hearts and minds?

4. Is turning to legalism like returning to the old covenant? Why do we sometimes find legalism enticing?

5. Do we put too much trust in human religious leaders? How? Why?

9
Once-For-All

*But now he has appeared once for all at the end of the ages
to do away with sin by the sacrifice of himself.*

Hebrews 9:26

We hate certain jobs, not because they are hard, but
because they won't stay done. Wouldn't it be great
if we could do things once-for-all? Mowing the grass is
not a real strain. The problem is, a week later it's time to
mow again. If only the grass would stay mowed! House
cleaning is thankless work, mainly because it is never
done. I detest shaving because I do it every day. Even
people who love to cook get tired of it because it is so
daily.

It happens in families, too. We don't really mind
correcting our children (after all, that's what parents are
for). What we mind is correcting them for the same things,
time after time. They don't particularly like it, either. What
causes the most strife in marriage are not the knock-down,
drag-out disagreements, but the little, annoying habits we
see in our husbands and wives each day.

Nothing stays done, nothing stays fixed, nothing
is once-for-all.

Not even, it seems the most important things. We
sincerely repent of sins only to fight them the next day.
Prayers don't stay prayed and the Bible doesn't stay read.
Our walk with God is precisely that: a walk that never
ends. Obedience is daily, not once-for-all.

But the most important event of all time happened once-for-all. The writer of Hebrews encourages us with the good news, the greatest news of all. Our salvation is permanent: complete, finished-once-for-all.

Christ's Sacrifice: Once for all

In the last chapter we saw how God's new deal includes the once-for-all salvation that comes through Jesus. The writer of Hebrews returns to this theme again and again. His encouraging word to us is that Christ's sacrifice is final and permanent.

> For Christ did not enter a man-made sanctuary that was only a copy of the true one; he entered heaven itself, now to appear for us in God's presence. Nor did he enter heaven to offer himself again and again, the way the high priest enters the Most Holy Place every year with blood that is not his own. Then Christ would have had to suffer many times since the creation of the world. But now he has appeared once for all at the end of the ages to do away with sin by the sacrifice of himself.

(Hebrews 9:24-26)

"Sacrifice" had a more concrete meaning to the original readers of Hebrews. When they heard "sacrifice" they thought of bleating sheep, bloody carcasses, and the smell of a slaughterhouse. They thought of Yom Kippur, the annual Day of Atonement, when the High Priest would take the blood of a sacrifice into the Most Holy Place. To them, sacrifice was blood and death and ritual, repeated year after year.

"Sacrifice" has a different meaning to contemporary people. We speak of sacrificing certain things for our children: giving up for their sake what we want. When I was twelve, my mother died. Dad was left alone with my younger brother Mark and me. He'd just received a promotion at work that meant he worked in the evening. Dad gave up his promotion to go back to the day shift, just so he could spend more time with Mark and me. He never got a chance at another promotion.

That was a sacrifice, one for which I will be eternally grateful. It cost Dad, but he did it willingly and joyfully. As much as I appreciate that sacrifice, it pales in comparison with those who have given their lives for others. Twenty years ago I had just begun teaching a group of teenagers on God's will for their lives. I didn't know the kids very well. One boy raised his hand and asked, "Suppose a boy and his dad went fishing and the boat turned over. They could only find one life jacket, so the dad put it on the boy. Help finally came, but by then the father had drowned. Does that mean the boy should grow up to be a preacher or something?"

"Where do they get these ideas?" I thought. But I said, "It doesn't mean the boy should be a preacher, and I don't think God took the boy's father away from him, but it might mean that God has a plan for that boy and wants him to follow him."

God must have been with me that day. He must have helped me answer that far-fetched hypothetical question, for (as you've probably guessed by now) it was not hypothetical. The boy who asked the question was the boy whose father drowned. His father sacrificed himself for him. Such sacrifices do not happen often; they occur more frequently in movies, books, and television than in real life. Yet occasionally one hears of someone who dies while rescuing someone else or who steps in front of a bullet meant for someone else or who pulls someone from the fire at the cost of his own life.

Such sacrifices are rare and noble. At the end of Charles Dickens' *Tale of Two Cities*, Sydney Carton has the opportunity to go to the guillotine in place of someone else. Carton has lived a wasted life, but now he has a chance to make his existence count for something. He says, "It is a far, far better thing I do, than I have ever done; it is a far, far better rest that I go to, than I have ever known." Even in literature, such sacrifices are rare and noble. They are even more so in real life.

Jesus sacrificed himself for us; we know that. We speak of it often. But do we realize the enormity of that sacrifice? God himself, in the flesh, saw his own flesh torn and bleeding. The creator of life felt his life ebb away. The one who invented pleasure felt the deepest pain. It was a far, far better thing than anyone had done before, or since, or ever. The very idea that God would die for sinners is enormous, unbelievable... not just rare, but absolutely unique.

The effect of Jesus' sacrifice is also enormous and unique. He took care of sin once, for all. My sin, your sin, the sins of the world—all the sins we have committed and all the sins we will commit. By his blood he cleanses our consciences so we may serve God.

> The blood of goats and bulls and the ashes of a heifer sprinkled on those who are ceremonially unclean sanctify them so they are outwardly clean. How much more, then, will the blood of Christ, who through the eternal Spirit offered himself unblemished to God, cleanse our consciences from acts that lead to death, so that we may serve the living God!

> (Hebrews 9:13-14)

Clean consciences—isn't that what we need? And don't we need them to stay clean? Whether animal or human, no sacrifices we make can cleanse us permanently. Only one sacrifice can and does: the sacrifice of the one who "entered the Most Holy Place once for all, by his own blood, having obtained eternal redemption" (Hebrews 9:12).

Eternal redemption, permanent cleansing, once-for-all, over and done—all for us. Can there be a more encouraging word?

Death and Judgment: Once for All

The writer of Hebrews moves quickly from this most encouraging word to two words that sound anything but encouraging: death and judgment.

> Just as man is destined to die once, and after that to face judgment, so Christ was sacrificed once to take away the sins of many people...

> (Hebrews 9:27-28)

Each person dies once. This isn't exactly late-breaking news, nor is it news we want to hear. Most of us make a great effort to ignore the fact that someday, we will die.

Why mention death here? Two reasons: the first is to highlight the finality of Jesus' sacrifice. He does not need to sacrifice himself again and again. His death was once-for-all because we all die once-for-all. The salvation he brings is, therefore, complete.

Secondly, the writer of Hebrews wants to remind us of our unavoidable deaths. Like Jesus, we, too, have an appointment with death, one we cannot escape. Why remind us of death? To get to judgment.

Judgment—it seems like the least encouraging word we could imagine. "Judgment" reminds us of the "hell-fire and brimstone" sermons of our youth. "Judgment" reminds us of our guilt. "Judgment" intensifies our already overwhelming fear of death.

What's "judgment" doing here? It's here to convince us not to fear death. This word of judgment is surrounded by words of salvation. Jesus died for our sins once-for-all, therefore death has lost its sting. "The sting of death is sin" (1 Corinthians 15:56). Jesus is coming again to bring salvation, so judgment does not mean condemnation. "There is now no condemnation for those who are in Christ Jesus" (Romans 8:1). We will die once, but we will live again in Christ. We come to judgment to be pronounced innocent by the blood of Christ.

In Christ, our greatest fears—death and judgment—disappear in victory, once-for-all. Death and judgment are not to be feared but embraced. They are no longer scary words, but words of encouragement.

Christ's Second Coming: Once for All

On the Day of Atonement the High Priest entered the Most Holy Place. While he was inside making sacrifices, the people waited outside the temple to see if he would return. They waited patiently to find out if God had accepted their sacrifice, to know if they truly were saved. When the High Priest reappeared, the people shouted with the joy of salvation.

Jesus has entered heaven with the sacrifice of his own blood. How can we be sure his sacrifice saves us? Because he will return from heaven to claim those who are his.

> ...[S]o Christ was sacrificed once to take away the sins of many people; and he will appear a second time, not to bear sin, but to bring salvation to those who are waiting for him.

> (Hebrews 9:28)

Jesus' second coming assures us of our salvation. More that that, he brings salvation when he comes.

"What does this mean?" you ask. "I thought Jesus brought salvation when he died for our sins? In what way is he still to bring it?"

To understand the answer we need to broaden our view of salvation. When we say, "Jesus saves," we usually mean he forgives our sins through his death. That's certainly true, but it doesn't exhaust the meaning of salvation. Our salvation is past; Jesus died for our sins. Our salvation is present; Jesus continues to forgive and transform us. But our salvation is also future, because our ultimate salvation is to be with Christ, to see him as he is, to serve God face-to-face. That will happen only when Christ comes again.

Many are confused about the Second Coming. They think our primary task is to try and figure out when the Lord will come, to read the signs of the time. The writer of Hebrews encourages us by saying the return of Christ is sure. We don't know when he will come but we know that he will come. The return of Christ is final, once-for-all. It puts an end to our struggles and marks the beginning of a new, transformed, glorious existence. It means salvation, being with our God and Savior forever. It's worth waiting for; that's why we're patient.

Life Between the Once-for-alls

Jesus came to die for us, once for all. He will return to bring us salvation, once for all. Now we live between that first and second coming. How should we live? What should we do?

Hebrews answers these questions. Between the first and second comings, we listen for the voice of Jesus, God's last word to humanity. God spoke in olden times in many and various ways. Now he speaks through his Son, one greater than angels. We dare not neglect that Son, that Word, that message, as we wait for his second coming.

We listen; we obey.

Between the first and second comings we rely on Jesus to help us. He is our brother, our champion who fights for us. He knows what it's like to be weak, to be tempted. He helps us when we are weak and tempted. He had to learn obedience, and through him we learn to obey.

Between the comings, we keep our hearts right. We do our spiritual exercise, to keep our faith alive. We trust the power and promises of God. We accept with joy the new deal God has made us, the new covenant that cost Jesus his blood. That new covenant is in our hearts and minds.

Life between the comings is a life of work. We work hard in all our tasks because we work for the Lord. Even when our work seems like slavery, we are told, "Whatever you do, work at it with all your heart, as working for the Lord, not for men..." (Colossians 3:23). Hebrews tells us more. The work we do between the comings is, itself, rest. We share in the rest of God. We look forward to that final rest we will enjoy when he comes.

Life between the comings looks back to Christ's once-for-all death on the cross for us. We are sure of our forgiveness. It is over, done with, final, permanent... once-for-all. We also look forward to the culmination of our salvation, that once-for-all return of our Savior.

We wait, we watch, and we pray. Someday we will see him: the one we're waiting for. Then we will be with him, once for all.

Questions for Discussion

1. Name some things you wish could be done once for all.

2. What are some sacrifices others have made for you? You have made for others? How do these compare to Jesus' sacrifice for us?

3. Since Jesus died to cleanse our consciences once for all, why do we sometimes feel guilty?

4. Is the Day of Judgment a frightening or a comforting thought to Christians?

5. If Jesus saves by his death, how can he bring salvation when he comes again?

10
Let Us...

You need to persevere so that when you have done the will of God, you will receive what he has promised.

Hebrews 10:36

Bible study at times can seem so sterile. We memorize facts, study people with strange names, and try to understand unfamiliar customs. When we finish the study, we may think, "So what? What does this really mean to my life on Monday morning? How does it change the way I live?"

We may especially feel that sense of sterility when we study Hebrews. It's a strange, unfamiliar book. It focuses on obscure characters like Melchizedek. It goes into great detail concerning the Old Testament sacrificial system—high priests, sacrifices, blood, and sanctuaries. It builds its case around unusual terms like "covenant," "mediator," and "tabernacle." Hebrews is considered one of the harder books of the New Testament, just because of its vocabulary.

But even when one masters the words and the Old Testament references in Hebrews, the question still remains: "So what?" Since Hebrews is a word of encouragement, its writer is very much concerned with the "so what." He is not writing a deep, theological volume to earn a degree or get a teaching post in a school. He is writing to real people, Christians who are under fire and in danger of despair. True, he goes into great detail about the new deal God had given them. He tells them—and us—perhaps more than we want to know about high priests and sacrifices. But he does all this to encourage us to action.

To put it differently, in Scripture the indicative always precedes the imperative. In other words, God always acts before he calls us to act. He changes our relationship to him before he tells us what to do. The Bible usually puts it in this form: "Since God has done this for you, here is what you should do for him and for others."

Hebrews also rehearses what God has done in order to spur believers to action.

> Therefore, brothers, since we have confidence to enter the Most Holy Place by the blood of Jesus, by a new and living way open to us through the curtain, that is, his body, and since we have a great high priest over the house of God, let us...

> (Hebrews 10:19-21)

Jesus has opened the way to God by sacrificing himself for us. The heavy curtain that separated Israel from the Most Holy Place was torn from top to bottom at the death of Christ (Matthew 27:51). The writer of Hebrews compares Christ's body to that curtain. His body was torn to give us free access to God.

Thus, Christian action begins with confidence in our salvation. This goes completely against some techniques of motivation one still sees in the church. Some church leaders believe one can only motivate Christians to service by playing on their guilt: "If you don't do these things then you're not faithful and you won't go to heaven." There is some truth in this statement; guilt and fear certainly can and sometimes should motivate us.

But a greater motivation is the love we have for God in response to his gracious gift of salvation. Jesus, our great High Priest, has taken care of our sins, once and for all. Now we have free access to God, unhindered by our sins. What does it mean to live in God's presence? The writer of Hebrews lists four responses to God's grace, each preceded by the phrase, "Let us...."

1. *Let Us Draw Near to God*

Jesus has opened the "new and living way" to God. The door to God stands wide open. The question remains: will we walk through that open door to deeper fellowship with God?

> [L]et us draw near to God with a sincere heart in full assurance of faith, having our hearts sprinkled to cleanse us from a guilty conscience and having our bodies washed with pure water.

> (Hebrews 10:22)

Through Jesus, God does all he can to draw us to him; he offers grace, full forgiveness, final sacrifice, and a new covenant. Now we must trust the grace of God. That trust or faith gives us full assurance that God is, that he cares, that he loves, that he forgives. Faith makes us sure of our salvation.

What makes us doubt our salvation? Our guilty consciences, maybe? We can't believe we're right with God because we know how much we fall short of what we should be. We sin; we are guilty to the bone—to the heart. What we need is to have our consciences cleaned, the stain of guilt removed.

In the Old Testament, animal blood was sprinkled on the people to cleanse their hearts and consciences (Hebrews 9:16-10:10), but they didn't stay clean. Now, Jesus cleanses our hearts and consciences permanently by his blood. When did that washing take place? When our bodies were washed with pure water—when we were baptized.

—Christ does!!

Baptism gives us full assurance of salvation. Some
react negatively to such a statement because they
misunderstand the significance of baptism. Baptism is not
magical; washing the body with water does no good unless
one gives the heart to God. Baptism is not a human work
that earns salvation. It is a work of God, a miracle that
makes our consciences pure. In baptism our hearts are
sprinkled with the blood of Christ and cleansed forever.

Why mention baptism here? Is the writer of
Hebrews telling his Christian readers they need to be
baptized again? Of course not. Instead, he is calling them
to draw near to God by reminding them of their baptism.
In baptism, they entered the new and living way to God,
the way opened by Jesus. They were being tempted to
turn back from that way, to drift from God. They needed
a reminder of what God had done for them, a reminder of
the pledge they made to God. They needed a reminder, an
assurance of salvation. They needed to remember their
baptism.

Paul does something similar when he writes the
Romans. Having given them full assurance of salvation,
he fears that some will say, "Shall we go on sinning that
grace may increase?" (Romans 6:1). Paul answers, "Of
course not," and then reminds them of their baptism.
Baptism both assures us of grace and motivates us to
obedience. In baptism, we died to sin. Therefore, we can
live in it no longer.

Do you remember when you were baptized? Do
you remember how clean you felt inside? Now, many
years later, many sins later, you may not feel as clean, but
you are. The blood of Christ continues to cleanse us after
baptism (1 John 1:7). It's not just that we *were* baptized,
we *are* baptized. The cleansing of baptism stays with us.
We are just as spiritually clean now as we were when we
came from the waters of baptism.

This full assurance of salvation draws us closer to God. We want to be closer, not to earn forgiveness of sins, but because he has already forgiven us.

Remember the story of the prodigal son in Luke 15? The son leaves home, wastes his inheritance, and finds himself feeding pigs. When he thinks of his father, he feels ashamed because he has a guilty conscience. But still he returns to his father. He returns because he has nowhere left to go. He expects to be a slave. But when the father sees him he welcomes him with open arms. He puts clothes on his back, a ring on his finger, and throws a party in his honor.

How much faster would the prodigal have returned if he'd known he'd be welcomed this way? In the same way, we are sure of our salvation. We are sure no barrier stands between us and a loving Father. Let us, therefore, run into his tender arms. Let us draw near to God.

2. *Let Us Hold Tight to Our Hope*

"I hope it doesn't rain tomorrow."

"I hope I make an 'A' on the test."

"I hope that bus driver knows what he's doing."

These are ways we use the word "hope" in daily conversation. "Hope" usually expresses a fond wish. It expresses our desires in situations where we have little control.

Biblical hope is something altogether different. When the Bible speaks of the hope of eternal life, it is more than just a fond wish. The Christian's hope is a sure thing, as sure as the promises of God.

> Let us hold unswervingly to the hope we profess, for he who promised is faithful.

> (Hebrews 10:23)

Once, when I was a kid, the leaders of our church decided to ask each member about his or her Christian hope. "If you died today, would you go to heaven?" they asked. A few answered, "No." They didn't have Christian hope. Most answered, "I hope so," meaning, "I'd like to think so." That's not Christian hope, either. Several answered, "Yes, I know I'd go to heaven."

"How do you know?" the leaders asked.

"Because I've gone to church all my life. I've been a good person and tried my best to do what the Bible says." They had hope but did not understand the basis for that hope. They didn't have Christian hope.

One lady answered, "Yes, I'm sure I'll go to heaven."

"What makes you so sure?" the leaders asked.

"Because God told me I will and I believe him."

That's Christian hope: a hope that is sure and strong, not because of what we have done, but because of what God has done. He has promised us eternal life through his Son, and he is a God who keeps his promises. So, no matter what we face, no matter what we do, even if we have little confidence in ourselves, we are sure of our hope. Our confidence is in God, not in what we see or how we feel or how spiritual we are. That hope is certain. Let us hold on to our hope.

As I write these words, I can look out my office window and see a balloon caught in a tree. It's the most tenacious balloon I've ever seen. Months ago, at the beginning of the winter, someone let go of the balloon and its string wrapped around the top branch of the tree. I watched it off and on, for several hours, expecting it to blow away. It was there the next day, and the next. Now, it's spring, the tree is blooming, the balloon has deflated, but it's still there. That balloon has been there through snow, ice, pouring rain, and gales of wind. It's still there—holding on.

We face spiritual wind, ice, and rain. All sorts of forces try to separate us from our hope, "the anchor for the soul" (Hebrews 6:19). Without hope, we would be blown away. Let us hold on to our hope.

3. *Let Us Spur One Another On*

I have an irritating friend. Actually, I have several irritating friends, but this one is especially irritating because he's always pushing me to examine my actions and motives. He serves as my external conscience, goading me on to be better than I am. I have other friends who do the same, not so much by word but by example. They are so good-natured. They serve others quietly, in countless ways. They give advice infrequently, but it's always wise. Such friends increase my faith and commitment.

It's easier to draw near to God and hold tight to our faith if we have such friends to help us. We also should move others to be closer to God.

And let us consider how we may spur one another on toward love and good deeds.

(Hebrews 10:24)

The Greek word translated "spur" or "provoke" in some translations can mean "irritate", or even refer to an attack of a high fever. It may seem strange for the writer of Hebrews to tell us to think up new ways to irritate our Christian brothers and sisters. But this is a peculiar kind of irritation. We "bug" one another, not to produce exasperation, but because of love. Out of our love for them we will not allow them to be less than what they can be. We insist they show their love for God by what they do. They insist we do the same. Let us spur one another on.

4.   *Let Us Not Give Up Meeting Together*

What is one obvious way we "bug" and encourage one another to love? By meeting together as Christians. When Christians assemble, they have several purposes in mind. The most important is to worship the Lord God. Another important purpose is to encourage one another in faith.

> Let us not give up meeting together, as some are in the habit of doing, but let us encourage one another—and all the more as you see the Day approaching.

> (Hebrews 10:25)

In my youth, this was the favorite proof text for condemning those who did not come to church regularly. Strangely enough, I most often heard those sermons at Sunday night and Wednesday night services, when much of the congregation was not present.

The writer of Hebrews wants his readers to meet together regularly, to "go to church." He specifically condemns those who have fallen into the habit of missing church—and it is a habit. We get busy and miss one service. Before we know it, we've missed another. Soon, we miss as often as we attend. Assembling with other Christians is crucial to maintaining our faith. If we give up the habit of meeting together, we can soon fall into a deliberate rejection of God's grace, a rejection that brings judgment (see Hebrews 10:26-31).

Is church attendance a legalistic duty? Not to the writer of Hebrews. Instead, like drawing near to God and holding on to our hope, it is a response to the amazing salvation Jesus brings. In light of what Jesus has done for us, we meet with fellow Christians to praise God and encourage one another. That encouragement reaches a peak of urgency as we look forward to the Second Coming of Jesus, that Day when we will see him as he is, and live with him forever. Let us meet to encourage one another.

Receiving What God Has Promised

Why did the Hebrews need so much encouragement to be faithful to God? Why do we need so much encouragement? Maybe because it's hard to stay faithful. It's hard because the world tells us we're crazy not to live by its values, because faithfulness demands day-after-day obedience, because life challenges us with boredom, work, pain, disappointment, and, finally, death.

At times we are tempted to give up, to throw away all the faith we've struggled for. In those times we hear the words of an encourager:

> So do not throw away your confidence; it will be richly rewarded. You need to persevere so that when you have done the will of God, you will receive what he has promised.

(Hebrews 10:35-36)

Don't give up. Remember what God has done for us. Draw near to him and hold tight to your hope when all seems hopeless. Remember, we're in this life of faithfulness together, so we meet to encourage and be encouraged; we hold to our confidence in a faithful God; we anticipate our eternal reward.

God calls us to his side. Let's go.

Questions for Discussion

1. In your experience, do Christians work harder when they think their salvation is in doubt or when they are confident of their salvation? Why? How does your church motivate its members for service?

2. How can baptism make us sure of salvation? do we place too much emphasis on baptism or too little?

3. What are some ways we can irritate each other to do good?

4. Why do some give up the habit of going to church?

11
Family Portrait

All these people were still living by faith when they died.
Hebrews 11:13

It usually happens in those old English movies: the setting is a stately manor or even a castle. The young lord of the manor is showing it to some visitors. They soon come to a long hall full of portraits.

"And here's great uncle Ruprecht," the young lord intones. "Fought Napoleon, you know... There's his mother, Henrietta. She hid the crown jewels for a spell during the troubles... This one is Beauregard. Bit of a rotter, actually. Didn't even go to battle in the Crimea."

And so it goes, portrait after portrait, until the tour is done. Before the movie is over you know the young lord himself will go to defend king and country. He will be sent off with instructions to be brave and uphold the family name. Of course, the greatest disgrace of all would be to put some blot upon the family crest by playing the coward; one must be faithful to long years of family tradition.

Our Family

The writer of Hebrews does something similar when he encourages his readers to be faithful to God. He leads them through the portrait gallery of faith, pointing out those heroes in Old Testament times who trusted God against all odds. Let's take a brief tour of that gallery.

Here is Abel. Murdered by his brother, Cain. A tragic figure? No. Rather he was a man of faith. By faith he offered an acceptable sacrifice to God. By faith he was commended as righteous. We know little about Abel, but we know the most important thing about him: he trusted God. Although murdered, his faith still echoes down the halls of time.

Then there's Enoch, who is even more obscure. All we know of Enoch is that he was not found because God took him. Because of his righteous life, he did not experience death—all through faith. *see JUDE 14*

Noah had faith: faith enough to believe God when he said he would send the flood. Faith enough to build an ark on dry land. Faith enough to enter the ark and gain salvation. He, too, had the righteousness that comes by faith.

Then there's the largest portrait of all: Abraham, The father of the faithful. God called him to go to a new land. Abraham went, not knowing where he was going. That took faith. He was promised this new land, but he never had it in his lifetime. Still, he trusted that God would give it to his children and grandchildren.

But he had no children and he and his wife Sarah were old. You can see Sarah, there in the background of the portrait. She and Abraham were practically dead, yet God promised them a son. They trusted that faithful God, *Heb 11:1* and so Isaac was born. From Isaac would come a better city and a great nation, as God had promised.

Then came the greatest test of Abraham's faith. God told him to kill his son, Isaac, the child of promise: not just to kill him, but to offer him as a sacrifice. It made no sense, but Abraham trusted God so much that he tied up Isaac, laid him on the altar, and raised the knife. Only then did God stop him. In a sense, Abraham received Isaac back from the dead—all because he trusted.

There's a group portrait next to Abraham. On the *to the right??* left is Isaac, in the middle, Jacob, and to the left, Joseph.

All three spoke of what God would do for the family after they died. They trusted God beyond death, beyond their ability to see.

The other large portrait in the gallery is of Moses. In the background one can view different scenes of his life: the basket where his parents hid him from the Egyptians, his choice to be with his people instead of living in Pharaoh's court. Then there's his return to Egypt, the plagues, culminating in the Passover, and Moses leading Israel through the dry land of the Red Sea. All this Moses accomplished by faith. The power was in God, not in Moses.

Other smaller portraits are scattered throughout the gallery: Rahab, Gideon, Barak, Samson, Jepthah, David, and Samuel. There's also a group picture of the prophets, portrayed as victorious conquerors, famous judges, and worthy martyrs—all by faith.

This is our genealogical tree, Our family album, Our heritage of faith, What does it mean to have faith, to be faithful, as they were faithful?

Our Character

Families many times share certain character traits. You may come from a talkative family or a quiet one. Some families hug more than others. Some have a long list of family traditions, while others have few. There are families full of outlaws and families full of lawmen. Insanity runs in some families, or so they say.

The distinctive characteristic of the family of God is faith. But what is faith? Hebrews gives one of the clearest descriptions of faith in the Bible:

> Now faith is being sure of what we hope for and certain of what we do not see.

(Hebrews 11:1)

"Sure of what we hope for." If there's one trait of all those we've seen in the gallery of faith, it's this: they all looked forward to something. Abel's life is cut short, but "by faith he still speaks, even though he is dead" (Hebrews 11:4). Death does not have the final word with Abel; he dies in hope. Abraham looks forward to a better country. Moses, Rahab, and all the rest hoped for something better. Faith made them sure of their hope.

To some, being sure of hope sounds like a contradiction. "Hope," to them, is merely a fond wish. Some even get upset with Christians or think we're foolish because we look forward to another, better world. They accuse us of being unrealistic and having our head in the clouds.

It is hard to be certain of our hope. Doubt comes to many of us. After all, day follows day, the world keeps on spinning, and things never change. What makes us think they ever will? Those we love grow ill and die. We place their bodies in the ground; it seems so final. What makes us think it's not? The rich get richer, the powerful more corrupt. The powerless suffer, the poor are cheated. It's always been that way. What makes us think things will ever be right? Faith.

Faith makes us certain of what we hope for, makes us certain the promises of God will come true, even though now it looks as though they have not. The heroes in the gallery of faith all looked forward to receiving what God had promised. They didn't get it, at least not fully—not in this life. Still, they trusted God's promises:

> All these people were still living by faith when they died. They did not receive the things promised; they only saw and welcomed them from a distance. And they admitted they were aliens and strangers on earth.

(Hebrews 11:13)

Believing God will give what he has promised sets us apart from other people. It makes us aliens and strangers. Some think we're strange because we see what they cannot see. That's what faith is: a new way of seeing. It makes us certain of what we do not see.

It's hard for people to admit there are realities they cannot see. Several years ago, my wife and I went for an eye exam. The optometrist was a friend of ours, so he examined us together. During my exam, my wife Deb mentioned that she thought I was colorblind. This excited my optometrist friend, since he'd given few color-blindness tests. He pulled down a book full of circles of multi-colored dots. You've probably seen these tests. Imbedded in the dots is a letter or number that most people can see.

I just saw dots.

"Can't you see the letter "A" there?" Deb asked.

"No," I replied.

Our optometrist friend reached in a drawer, pulled out a red lens, and said, "Here, try this." I looked through the lens and, sure enough, the letter "A" was there, as big as life.

It's disconcerting to know there are things you cannot see. Particularly when others see them. But faith is like the red lens; it shows us what we cannot see without it. It shows us the hand of God.

In the routines of life, it's hard to see the hand of God. In the tragedies of life, it's even harder. Abel is murdered. Abraham has to leave his homeland. Isaac is bound on the altar. Israel is enslaved in Egypt. Prophets are martyred. Where is God in all this?

He is there, calling, working, and saving. But we cannot see his work with the naked eye. These heroes from the portrait gallery saw him by faith. They saw him in the routines and the tragedies of life. They trusted and were sure of his promises. Even when those promises did not come true in their lifetimes, still they trusted. They died in faith.

This is our family heritage. When life caves in for us or when we face another day much like the day before, we do not lose hope. Faith makes us sure of what we hope for. When others think us strange because we don't live for pleasure, don't promote ourselves, or because we sacrificially care for others, we are happy to be strange and alien. We see what others do not. Faith makes us certain of what we don't see with our eyes, certain that the Unseen God holds us in his loving hand—certain his promises are true.

Our Endurance

However, it's not always easy to maintain our certainty when others think us strange and alien. It's particularly difficult if the strange looks they give us turn to active discrimination and persecution. What we need is a good memory. We need to remember who we are, reflect on our heritage of faith, and recall the devotion we had when we first came to Christ. Even before he takes us through the gallery of faith, the writer of Hebrews says:

> Remember those earlier days after you had received the light, when you stood your ground in a great contest in the face of suffering.

> So do not throw away your confidence; it will be richly rewarded. You need to persevere so that when you have done the will of God, you will receive what he has promised. For in just a very little while,

> "He who is coming will come and will not delay.

> But my righteous one will live by faith.
> And if he shrinks back, I will not be pleased
> with him."

> But we are not of those who shrink back and are
> destroyed, but of those who believe and are saved.

(Hebrews 10:32, 35-39)

In times of trial our faith must endure. We build that endurance by remembering the confidence we had at the beginning of our discipleship. Do you recall the day you were saved? Most of us can remember that moment: the thrill, the certainty, the seriousness of our commitment. When our faith is challenged, we must recapture that time.

In times of trial we relive past battles we have won, contests where we stood our ground by faith. Can you remember a time when temptation was strong, but still you endured? Can you remember how Christ stood beside you in that ordeal? Is he not still standing beside us?

We build endurance by recalling our family character. We tour the gallery of faith and claim Enoch, Abraham, Sarah, Joseph, Rahab, and others as our spiritual ancestors. This is one reason we need to study our Bibles, to see the family tree of faith.

Most of all, we build endurance by looking to Jesus, the champion of faith.

> Therefore, since we are surrounded by such a great cloud of witnesses, let us throw off everything that hinders and the sin that so easily entangles, and let us run with perseverance the race marked out for us. Let us fix our eyes on Jesus, the author and perfecter of our faith, who for the joy set before him endured the cross, scorning its shame, and sat down at the right hand of the throne of God. Consider him who endured such opposition from

sinful men, so that you will not grow weary and lose heart.

(Hebrews 12:1-3)

To encourage endurance, the writer of Hebrews uses three word pictures. First, he says the Christian life is a wrestling match where we must hold our ground. We recall earlier victories and so do not lose heart. Next, the Christian life is participation in the family of faith. We imitate the faith of our spiritual ancestors. Finally, the Christian life is a race. Not a sprint, but a marathon requiring long endurance. Our spiritual ancestors who have finished the race are there to cheer us on.

Most importantly, Jesus is there to cheer us on. We keep our eyes fixed on him, standing at the finish line. He knows what it's like to endure: he endured the cross. He knows what it's like to be a stranger, to be taunted, and to be ridiculed. He endured and despised that shame. He knows what it's like to finish the race, to win and to receive the award. As we saw in an earlier chapter, he is the author—or, better—the champion of our faith. He fights for us and runs with us. He's there to give us the crown of victory.

His is the greatest portrait in the gallery of faith, greatest because we see his face in all the other portraits. Abel, Abraham, Moses, and Sarah all resemble him, for he alone is the ultimately faithful one. He is our family. We imitate his faith. We have his character. Through him, we are sure of what we hope for, certain of what we cannot see.

In him we endure.

Questions for Discussion

1. Of all the heroes of faith in Hebrews 11 who is your favorite? Why?

2. How do these examples illustrate faith as being sure of what we hope for?

3. How do faith and hope relate to the promises of God? When did these people receive what God promised?

4. What are some things we see by faith that others cannot see?

5. In what ways are these heroes and Jesus examples of endurance?

12
A Consuming Fire

"Therefore since we are receiving a kingdom that cannot be shaken, let us be thankful, and so worship God acceptably with reverence and awe, for 'Our God is a consuming fire.'"
Hebrews 12:28-29

Is fire good, or bad? On the one hand, fire, in different forms, keeps us warm in the winter. It saves countless people from freezing to death. Fire cooks our food, produces the electricity that runs our machines, and forges the metal and bricks that make up our buildings. It's hard to imagine life without fire.

On the other hand, fire is the most destructive force in all creation. It can consume forests, houses, families, and entire cities.

My wife's family knows the power of fire. Years ago, while on a camping trip, a kerosene lantern that was supposed to harness fire instead exploded, spreading flames throughout the tent. Most of the family escaped the tent with minor burns. Two others had more serious injuries. My wife's sister, Gwen, saw the tent burn down around her.

The family wasn't sure Gwen would survive. But she did, by God's grace. Not only did she survive, but she prospered. Now she is married, with children of her own.

Gwen's scars are real, but the whole family was scarred inside by the experience. They know the power of fire.

The Fire That Punishes

There are few "God is" statements in the New Testament. Among our favorites: "God is Spirit" (John 4:24), "God is faithful" (2 Corinthians 1:18), "God is just" (2 Thessalonians 1:6), "God is light" (1 John 1:5), and "God is love" (1 John 4:8).

Hebrews says, "God is a consuming fire" (Hebrews 12:29). Is that one of our favorites? Probably not.

"Consuming fire" calls forth images we'd rather forget: hell, eternal punishment, and memories of sermons that painted the horrors of torment so clearly we could almost smell the smoke and hear the cries of the damned.

"I don't believe in a God who would condemn people to hell for eternity," some say. At first it may seem like a noble sentiment to refuse to believe in a vengeful God.

But what kind of God do we want? Do we really want a God who does not punish sin, who ignores those who murder the innocent? Do we really want an indulgent Father who can look at all the horrors that humans inflict on each other and say, "It's no big deal. Boys will be boys."

I don't think so. Even the most tolerant of us think some deserve punishment from God: Hitler, mass murderers, serial killers, or those who prey on children.

We want to reserve hell for only the worst of cases—that is, only for those worse than we are.

There is a wideness in God's mercy, but he is also a just and holy God who hates sin. He is quick to forgive but will not forgive those who continue to reject him— even those who are not mass murderers.

"What kind of God do we want?" is really not the question. We do not get to choose our gods, or, if we do, they are mere idols. The true and living God will be who he is, whether we like it or not.

And he is a terrifying, punishing God.

He leads Israel from Egyptian slavery to the foot of Mount Sinai. There he appears to them in smoke and fire (Exodus 19:17-19). God terrifies Israel. Why? Is he a mean God who frightens us like a bully frightens little children? No, he is frightening because he is God, the Almighty, the thrice-holy.

Most frightening is his love. He appears to Israel at Sinai not just to frighten them but to give them his covenant of love. But God's love is demanding. He demands that Israel love and serve him only—that is the first command. He is a jealous God; he allows no rivals. His fiery punishment breaks out on all who reject him for another. As Moses told Israel:

> Be careful not to forget the covenant of the Lord your God that he made with you; do not make for yourselves an idol in the form of anything the Lord your God has forbidden. For the Lord your God is a consuming fire, a jealous God.

> (Deuteronomy 4:23-24)

This word of warning is not just for ancient Israel. It is for us who follow God today. Hebrews has already told us of the new covenant, the better deal God has made with us. We too dare not forget that covenant and turn to the gods of our age—wealth, comfort, power, and success. To do so invites the punishing fire of a jealous God, as Hebrews makes clear by quoting Deuteronomy (Hebrews 12:29). The prophet Isaiah uses even stronger language in his warning:

> The sinners in Zion are terrified; trembling grips the godless:

> "Who of us can dwell with the consuming fire?"
> "Who of us can dwell with everlasting burning?"

> (Isaiah 33:14)

How do we square a punishing, terrifying, fiery God with the God who is love? Don't these descriptions of God remind us of "Sinners in the Hands of an Angry God," a sermon by the eighteenth century preacher Jonathan Edwards? Most of us read the sermon in high school literature class. Perhaps you remember how Edwards described God as holding us like a spider suspended by a thin thread over the eternal flame. "God loathes us," Edwards said. Maybe you remember your reaction to that sermon.

No doubt, Edward's rhetoric is extreme. However we can't ignore the biblical teaching that God punishes sin. He punishes, not because he loathes us, but because he loves us. He loves us so much that he wants us for himself alone. If we refuse him, the fiery love of God is seen as punishment.

The Fire that Disciplines

God even punishes those who love him, but in that case it is not called punishment, but discipline. Again, God's love is not all sweetness and light. It is a love that demands all from us. This is good news, a word of encouragement: God treats us as his children.

And have you forgotten that word of encouragement that addresses you as sons:

> "My son, do not make light of the Lord's discipline,
> and do not lose heart when he rebukes you,
> because the Lord disciplines those he loves,
> and he punishes everyone he accepts as a son."

(Hebrews 12:5-6)

Discipline... That word also may bring back painful memories. When I was a kid, my parents were mean and cruel to me. I wanted to eat hot dogs and sweets—candy, cookies, and cake. Instead, they made me eat vegetables. When we went to the store, I always wanted a new toy. Sometimes they bought me one, but other times they refused, saying, "You have enough toys at home." More than once they took me to the doctor, knowing that I was to get a painful shot. At age five, things got worse. They made me go to school, against my will. In later years, when I wanted to play outside until bedtime, they forced me to come in and do my homework. In addition to all this, they gave me many a "whuppin" (as we say in the South), when I disobeyed them.

It's hard to imagine any parents who were more cruel than mine... Of course, by now you've caught on: they were not cruel at all; they loved me. And because they loved me they made me eat my vegetables, take my shots, and go to school. Because they loved me they did not give me everything I wanted. Because they loved me they disciplined me.

I didn't always appreciate it at the time. I even thought them cruel and mean. But now, looking back, I realize what I mistook for cruelty was love.

God treats his children the same way.

Endure hardship as discipline; God is treating you as sons. For what son is not disciplined by his father? If you are not disciplined (and everyone undergoes discipline), then you are illegitimate children and not true sons. Moreover, we have all had human fathers who disciplined us and we respected them for it. How much more should we submit to the Father of our spirits and live! Our fathers disciplined us for a little while as they thought best; but God disciplines us for our good that we might share in his holiness.

(Hebrews 12:7-10)

How does God discipline us? Through hardship. I don't think this means that all the bad things that happen to us are sent directly from God. Sometimes hardship is just part of being human. Sometimes it's the result of sin. Sometimes it's sent by the devil. Whatever the source of hardship, God can use it for our good. He uses the suffering and pain of life to discipline us, to teach us what is truly important, to move us to trust him alone. Like our parents, he disciplines out of love.

If you were really treated cruelly by your parents, then it may be hard to understand God's discipline. Our parents disciplined us "as they thought best." They didn't always do it right. If you're a parent, you know how difficult it is to discipline your children right, to strike the correct balance between being too strict or too lenient. We do the best we can. God's discipline, however, is perfect. It is always "for our good." It is intended to lead us to holiness.

It doesn't always seem that way. We all cry out at times, "God, why is this happening to me?" We wonder how a loving Father can treat us this way. As Hebrews says:

> No discipline seems pleasant at the time, but painful. Later on, however, it produces a harvest of righteousness and peace for those who have been trained by it.
>
> (Hebrews 12:11)

We may mistakenly think God wants us to be happy—now. Instead, he wants us to be holy now, so we will be truly happy later. As Christians, we are in training. As we run the marathon of the Christian life, God keeps us in shape through his discipline. We don't like hardship. We don't like pain. As a kid I didn't like vegetables, shots, and homework. But they were good for me.

God is a fire. He burns us with the fire—the pain—of hardship. He does it out of love, to discipline us: to make us strong and holy, to give us peace and righteousness, to make us his and his alone.

The Fire That Purifies

Our God is a consuming fire. He consumes the wicked in punishment. He disciplines those whom he loves. He also purifies his people by fire, consuming the sin and evil within them.

The prophet Isaiah has a vision of God enthroned in glory. In the presence of this holy God, Isaiah knows his own sinfulness:

> "Woe to me!" I cried. "I am ruined! For I am a man of unclean lips, and I live among a people of unclean lips and my eyes have seen the King, the lord Almighty."
>
> Then one of the seraphs flew to me with a live coal in his hand, which he had taken with tongs from the altar. With it he touched my mouth and said, "See, this has touched your lips; your guilt is taken away and your sin is atoned for."
>
> (Isaiah 6:5-7)

Isaiah sees the Consuming Fire, then he is purified by it. Later in the prophets, the coming Messiah is spoken of as one who will purify and refine by fire.

> But who can endure the day of his coming? Who can stand when he appears? For he will be like a refiner's fire or a launderer's soap. He will sit as a refiner and purifier of silver; he will purify the Levites and refine them like gold and silver.
>
> (Malachi 3:2-3)

We often speak of Christ as the one who cleanses us and washes away our sins. We sing, "Are You Washed in the Blood?" and "Whiter than Snow" (or, at least, we used to sing them). We don't sing, "Are You Refined in the Fire?" or "Purer than Silver." Perhaps the idea of being refined by fire sounds more painful than washing. Fire hurts, but the hurt can be good for us.

Purification by fire works much like discipline. The pain and suffering are real, but are good for us. God's love is a fire: it consumes what it cannot purify and purifies what will not be destroyed. Peter puts it this way:

> In this you greatly rejoice, though now for a little while you may have had to suffer grief in all kinds of trials. These have come so that your faith—of greater worth than gold, which perishes even though refined by fire—may be proved genuine and may result in praise, glory and honor when Jesus Christ is revealed.
>
> (1 Peter 1:6-7)

In the presence of the Holy God, in the face of trial and grief, we face a fire. That fire can warm us, cleanse us, and purify us, or it can punish and destroy. The choice is ours.

An Encouraging Word?

Talk of fire may not seem encouraging, but the writer of Hebrews intends it to be. He reminds his readers of the fire of God on Mount Sinai. He tells of God's promise to shake earth and heaven once more at the end of time. All this talk of fire and earthquake is meant to encourage. We have a kingdom that cannot be shaken. We have a faith that is purified, not destroyed, by fire. We react to the gift of that unshakable kingdom by worshipping God.

Therefore, since we are receiving a kingdom that cannot be shaken, let us be thankful and so worship God acceptably with reverence and awe, for our God is a consuming fire.

(Hebrews 12:28-29)

Reverence... Awe... Fear... This is how we approach God. Not just fear of a punishing fire, but respect for the fire that disciplines and refines us. We serve a God we cannot control. We dare not try to manipulate him. Instead, we fall at his feet, unworthy and unclean. He sends his fire to cleanse us. He raises us to our feet to worship, adore, and serve him forever. We burn with the fire of his love.

Questions for Discussion

1. Is fire good or bad? What makes it good or bad?

2. Why is it we hear so few lessons on God as a consuming fire? Do we need to hear more? Are such lessons positive and uplifting or do they do harm?

3. What are some ways God disciplines us? Does he ever send bad times to make us better?

4. Should we ask God to discipline us more? Should we pray for hardship, not for an easy path in life?

5. What is reverence? Awe? Have we lost these attitudes as Christians? If so, how can we recover them?

13
Last Words

"My friends, I have written only a short letter to encourage you, and I beg you to pay close attention to what I have said."

Hebrews 13:22 (CEV)

Do you ever run out of time before you finish what you want to say? Maybe it's on the phone, when you have to hang up or take another call. Perhaps it's face-to-face, when another appointment looms. It can even happen in a letter, when the letter carrier is at the door and you want to get it off today. At times, we all have to rush our words. That doesn't mean we don't mean them. Indeed, they may even be vitally important.

That's the way the last chapter of Hebrews feels. It's as if the writer is out of time or paper, or the messenger who is to carry the letter is at the door. I guess that's why Hebrews packs so much into this last chapter. Having spent twelve chapters encouraging the Hebrews (in what he calls a brief letter), the writer has eight more things to quickly add to his list of encouraging words. Although he sounds rushed, he has vital things to say.

Love and Care for Others

Having reminded us of the fiery love of God, the writer urges that we show that same love to others. In the Bible, Christian love is always more than an emotion: it is an action. Love must be shown; love must be done.

Keep on loving each other as brothers. Do not forget to entertain strangers, <u>for by so doing some</u> <u>people have entertained angels without knowing</u> <u>it.</u> Remember those in prison as if you were their fellow prisoners, and those who are mistreated as if you yourselves were suffering.

(Hebrews 13:1-3)

Love for one another has always been a sign of true discipleship. Jesus said, "All men will know that you are my disciples if you love one another" (John 13:35).

But if love is an action, not just an attitude, how do we show it? Hebrews gives two concrete ways of displaying love for our fellow Christians. One is hospitality. In the first century, when Christians traveled from place to place doing the Lord's work, there were no hotel chains competing for their business. One had to stay in the houses of strangers: fellow Christians that one had not met.

It takes a great deal of trust to let a stranger into your home. It's always a bother, <u>but it's a sign of Christian</u> <u>love, even today.</u> I write this a week after speaking at a campaign for Christ in London. I took the overnight flight from the U.S., arrived at Heathrow airport, and was driven to the house where I was staying. These wonderful people, the Cleer family, welcomed me into their home and even gave me a key to the front door. Think of that in this day and age—giving a stranger a key to your house!

But I was not just a stranger, I was their brother in Christ. They showed their love for me by disrupting their routine, by giving up a bed for me and sleeping on the floor, and by trusting me with the front door key. Their love was real; it was love in action. That's the kind of brotherly love we are called to have. Who knows? We <u>might even be entertaining angels as Abraham did</u> (Genesis 18:1-8)—although the Cleers will tell you, I was no angel.

The other expression of love Hebrews mentions is caring for those in prison. Christians in the first century were sometimes subjected to imprisonment because of their faith. Some of the readers of Hebrews had been imprisoned.

> Remember the earlier days after you had received the light, when you stood your ground in a great contest in the face of suffering. Sometimes you were publicly exposed to insult and persecution; at other times you stood side by side with those who were so treated. You sympathized with those in prison and joyfully accepted the confiscation of your property, because you knew you had better and lasting possessions.

(Hebrews 10:32-34)

Some of the Hebrew Christians were in prison. Those who were not are called to sympathize with them. But Christian sympathy, like Christian love, is more than an emotion; it means specific action. They were to care for those in prison, to "remember them." In the Bible, when God remembers his people, he acts on their behalf. To remember those in prison means to visit them: to bring them food, comfort, and anything else they need. Such love is dangerous. One might find himself sharing a cell with those he comes to visit. But that is our calling.

Visiting strangers and prisoners reminds us of that great judgment scene Jesus paints for us. On the last day he will judge us according to whether or not we fed the hungry, clothed the naked, took in the stranger, and visited the prisoner. To care for our brothers and sisters whom Jesus calls the "least of these" is to care for Jesus himself (Matthew 25:31-46). "The King will reply, 'I tell you the truth, whatever you did for the least of these brothers of mine, you did for me'" (Matthew 25: 40). By loving each other we show our love for him.

Keep Marriage Holy

The temptation to break our marriage vows is nothing new. The Hebrews faced pressure from without—imprisonment and loss of goods—but they also faced those internal pressures we all face. The question we have to answer, along with them is: will we be faithful to one another and to God?

> Marriage should be honored by all, and the marriage bed kept pure, for God will judge the adulterer and the sexually immoral.
>
> (Hebrews 13:4)

Be faithful to your husband or wife. Why? Because God will get you if you don't. That's what Hebrews says. At first, it may seem like a bad motivation to faithfulness. Should we really avoid adultery just out of fear of punishment?

No, there are other reasons. We made a vow in marriage and we are people who keep our promises. We love our wives, our husbands. We have children to care for. Adultery invites embarrassment, heartbreak, disease, pain, and death.

And there's hell, too. Our God is a consuming fire. If we are being singed by the flames of illicit passion, it's possible nothing moves us back toward faithfulness more than this: our marriage is before God. Our vow is to him, not just to our spouse. If we are unfaithful to our marriage partner, we are unfaithful to God. Even a word of judgment can be a word of encouragement.

Trust God, Not Money

Besides adultery, another perennial temptation is greed.

Keep your lives free from the love of money and be content with what you have, because God has said,

"Never will I leave you;
never will I forsake you."

So we say with confidence,

"The Lord is my helper; I will not be afraid.
What can man do to me?"

(Hebrews 13:5,6)

Few Christians of my acquaintance will admit to greed—loving money. Yet many of us, if we are honest, have to admit we want more money... just a little more. We are not content with what we have. We trust our bank accounts, mutual funds, retirement savings, and real estate equity; we think they will protect us from financial harm and ruin.

Only one truly protects. If our trust is in him, then no one, nothing can harm us.

Remember Your Leaders

To be faithful requires help from God but also help from fellow Christians. There are those who preceded us in the faith and have proved themselves faithful through long years of obedience. The lives of these leaders demand imitation, respect, and obedience.

Remember your leaders, who spoke the word of God to you. Consider the outcome of their way of life and imitate their faith.

Obey your leaders and submit to their authority.
They keep watch over you as men who must give
account. Obey them so that their work will be a
joy, not a burden, for that would be of no advantage
to you.

(Hebrews 13:7, 17)

Obeying God is hard enough; obeying human
leaders in the church is harder, because they are human
and fallible. Still, we are called to obey. Why? Why should
we submit to any human authority?

Because true church leaders get their authority
from Jesus, the one who taught his disciples, "whoever
wants to be great among you must be your servant" (Mark
10:43). We obey our leaders because they serve us. We
obey because they have lived lives worthy of imitation.
We obey because it is to our advantage. They are watching
out for us; their authority is the power of love.

Trust Grace, Not Legalism

We need to trust our leaders because there are
strange teachings out there. God's people are always in
danger of trading grace for ritual, ceremony, and legalism.

Do not be carried away by all kinds of strange
teachings. It is good for our hearts to be
strengthened by grace, not by ceremonial foods,
which are of no value to those who eat them.

Let us, then, go to him outside the camp, bearing
the disgrace he bore. For here we do not have an
enduring city, but we are looking for the city that
is to come.

(Hebrews 13:9, 13-14)

The particular type of legalism here—eating ceremonial, kosher food—may not tempt us. However, relying on external obedience instead of faith is a perpetual temptation. Faith may bring disgrace in the eyes of the world. It may even disgrace us with some legalists in the church. No matter; we share the disgrace of Jesus. Legalism looks outward, to rules and regulations. Faith is strange to some because it looks forward, to an enduring city still to come. We should not look back to the old way—salvation by rules—that was no salvation at all. We should look forward to the salvation that comes by grace through faith.

Offer the Sacrifices of Praise and Service

Jesus has offered himself as the once-for-all sacrifice for sin. We can add nothing to that sacrifice. Through him our sins are completely forgiven. Nothing we can do can earn that salvation. It is by grace, not works.

Yet there are sacrifices we make in response to the sacrifice of Christ.

> Through Jesus, therefore, let us continually offer to God a sacrifice of praise—the fruit of lips that confess his name. And do not forget to do good and to share with others, for with such sacrifices God is pleased.

> (Hebrews 13:15-16)

We praise God through Jesus. We confess his name. We also express our praise by doing good and sharing with others. This is the essence of living by faith.

Rely on God

Love and serve others. Be faithful in marriage. Do not trust money. Obey your leaders. Stay with grace. Sacrifice to God.

It sounds like a list of do's and don'ts for Christians. It may even sound like the worst of legalism: we are right with God if we keep the rules.

But Hebrews is no legalist document. It gives a word of encouragement, not a burdensome list of commands. What keeps the list from becoming legalism? The writer relies on God to give the power to obey.

> May the God of peace, who through the blood of the eternal covenant brought back from the dead the Lord Jesus, that great Shepherd of the sheep, equip you with everything good for doing his will, and may he work in us what is pleasing to him, through Jesus Christ, to whom be glory for ever and ever. Amen.

> (Hebrews 13:20-21)

In ourselves, we lack the power to be always loving, always obedient, always faithful. But God has that power. He had power enough to raise Jesus from the dead. His same resurrection power is at work in us. It equips us. It empowers us to do what is pleasing to God.

Here is an encouraging word! God himself is with us. He keeps his commands in us. We only have to trust, to rest, to rely on his power—not our own. That is faith.

Continue to Follow the Unchanging Jesus

In the middle of his closing advice to the Hebrews, the author makes a statement that does not seem to fit:

> Jesus Christ is the same yesterday and today and forever.
>
> (Hebrews 13:8)

Why bring this up in the context of being faithful in marriage, obeying leaders, showing hospitality, and praising God?

Because it is the ultimate word of encouragement. In a culture grown violent and cold, the love of Jesus is constant. It moves us to constancy in our love for others. In an age that does not respect experience and authority, the unchanging leadership of Jesus shines through. It motivates us to obey our spiritual leaders. In a time when many marriages fail, the faithfulness of Jesus, who is always the same, gives us the power to be consistently faithful in marriage. *Highest divorce rate is among Christians in Bible Belt*

The hurried, staccato nature of this last chapter should not blind us to the power of this short phrase: "Jesus Christ is the same." Christian readers of the book then and now are tempted in their walk of faith. What can we do to continue to follow the path of God?

When surrounded by bewildering claims to truth, what do we do? We remember Jesus Christ, God's last Word to humanity. When life caves in and all seems hopeless, where do we turn? To Jesus Christ, the one who helps us more than angels. When others just don't understand, who is it who can feel most deeply with us? The flesh-and-blood Jesus. When we fail miserably, who can heal and make things right? Our great High Priest and Savior.

So what do we do in hard times? We walk with

Most abortions (70%) are from Christians

Jesus. Everyone else abandons us. We walk on. Sickness and death attack. We walk on. We disappoint others and ourselves. We walk on. We grow weary to our bones. We walk on.

We walk on because there is one who has always walked with us. Jesus Christ is the same. His companionship is certain. He is the same yesterday. He led us in the past. In all our times of trouble, in all our times of joy, we can look back and see his loving hand.

We walk on because Jesus Christ is the same tomorrow. There will come a day when every knee bows to him and every tongue confesses his name. There will come a day when we will walk with him not by faith but by sight. We will see him as he is. We will be with him forever.

May that day come quickly!

Questions for Discussion

1. What are some concrete ways we show love to others?

2. List ten reasons why we should be faithful in marriage. What reason does Hebrews give?

3. What is the primary role of leaders in the church? How should we follow them?

4. How are praise and service sacrifices to God?

5. How is the "sameness' of Jesus an encouraging word to us?